Failing Liberty 101

The Hoover Institution gratefully acknowledges
the following individuals and foundations
for their significant support of the
***Boyd and Jill Smith Task Force
on Virtues of a Free Society:***

BOYD AND JILL SMITH
WILLIAM E. SIMON FOUNDATION

The Hoover Institution gratefully acknowledges

ROBERT AND MARION OSTER

for their significant support of this publication.

Failing Liberty 101

How We Are Leaving Young Americans
Unprepared for Citizenship in a Free Society

William Damon

HOOVER INSTITUTION PRESS
STANFORD UNIVERSITY   STANFORD, CALIFORNIA

The Hoover Institution on War, Revolution and Peace, founded
at Stanford University in 1919 by Herbert Hoover, who went
on to become the thirty-first president of the United States, is
an interdisciplinary research center for advanced study on
domestic and international affairs. The views expressed in
its publications are entirely those of the authors and do not
necessarily reflect the views of the staff, officers, or Board of
Overseers of the Hoover Institution.

www.hoover.org

Hoover Institution Press Publication No. 611

Hoover Institution at Leland Stanford Junior University,
Stanford, California 94305-6010

First printing 2011
17 16 15 14 13 12 11   7 6 5 4 3 2 1

Manufactured in the United States of America

The paper used in this publication meets the minimum
Requirements of the American National Standard for
Information Sciences—Permanence of Paper for Printed
Library Materials, ANSI/NISO Z39.48-1992. ♾

Cataloging-in-Publication Data is available from
the Library of Congress.
ISBN-13: 978-0-8179-1364-9 (cloth. : alk. paper)
ISBN-13: 978-0-8179-1366-3 (e-book)

*To Dick and Sue Jacobsen
for their friendship, support,
and good work in education.*

CONTENTS

FOREWORD

The Hoover Institution's Boyd and Jill Smith Task Force on Virtues of a Free Society aims to clarify the beliefs, practices, and institutions that play a crucial role in forming and sustaining liberty, and a distinctly American way of life. By examining the political thought and culture of the American founding, the historical evolution of government and society, and changing public opinion, the group will reflect on the fabric of our civil society. The current core membership of the task force includes Peter Berkowitz, Gerard V. Bradley, David Brady, James W. Ceaser, William Damon, Robert P. George, Tod Lindberg, Harvey C. Mansfield, Russell Muirhead, Clifford Orwin, and Diana Schaub.

In this volume, *Failing Liberty 101*, William Damon explores the links between virtue and liberty in our young population of American citizens. Damon's research argues that the adult community (parents, educators, intellectuals, and public leaders) is failing to prepare the next generation to be responsible citizens and that unless we pay attention and meet the challenge as stewards of a priceless heritage, our nation and the future prospects of all will suffer.

John Raisian
Tad and Dianne Taube Director
Hoover Institution, Stanford University

ACKNOWLEDGMENTS

This book was written in connection with the Boyd and Jill Smith Task Force on Virtues of a Free Society at the Hoover Institution on War, Revolution and Peace. I thank Boyd and Jill Smith for their generous support of the task force's efforts and for their interest in the work that I present in this book. Peter Berkowitz and David Brady have been the task force co-chairs, and I thank them and the other members for the many good insights and constructive comments that they offered me during my presentations of the preliminary chapter drafts. I am also grateful to John Raisian, David Davenport, Denise Elson, and Marianne Jacobi for the extremely helpful support and assistance they have given me during my task force work.

In my office at Stanford, Heather Malin, Parissa Jahromi, and Brandy Quinn have helped me conduct the research on American identity and civic purpose that I have described in this book. Heather has contributed to the manuscript in other ways as well, including organizing comments, reviewing library sources, and convening discussion groups. Elissa Hirsh has given me able assistance in checking references and other editorial tasks.

Many of the quotations from American leaders that I cite throughout the chapters of this book are drawn from a list compiled by David Gowdy, president of the Washington, Jefferson & Madison Institute, and passed along to me by Dr. John M. Templeton Jr., president of the John Templeton Foundation. The Foundation also supported the June 2010 American Identity Renewed conference that I refer to in Chapter 4 of the book. I also thank Dr. Templeton and Kent Hill, vice president for character development at the foundation, for the valuable ideas and gracious feedback they have provided as I have pursued this line of inquiry.

INTRODUCTION

*Liberty can no more exist without virtue . . . than the body can
live and move without a soul.   —John Adams*

Whenever we speak about the future of any society, we
are really speaking about today's young and their
upcoming prospects. Preparing young people for bright
futures is one of the core obligations of every adult community. Of course, this means providing the young people with
the vocational skills they will need to prosper. But vocational skills alone are not sufficient. Beyond such skills,
there are qualities of character that determine the success or
failure of a person's life. Foremost among these qualities are
the virtues that make possible a life of honor and integrity.

To ensure a bright future for young people and the society they will inherit, every adult community must take seriously its responsibility to raise young people for lives of
virtue. Failure to do so inevitably will result in societal dec-
adence—literally, a "falling away," from the Latin *decadere*.
World history has shown us time and again what happens
to a society when its citizens no longer prize virtue. Citizens

1

have an obligation to preserve the benefits of their societies for the future as well as the present—which means an obligation to foster virtuous character in the young. Preparing young people for responsible citizenship in a free society is a crucial part of this obligation for adult citizens in the United States.

This book's main message is disclosed in its title: at the present time, we are failing to meet this obligation for major sectors of our youth population, to the detriment of their life prospects and those of liberty and democracy in our society. The problems I discuss in this book—a decline in civic purpose and patriotism, a crisis of faith, a rise in cynicism, self-absorption, ignorance, and indifference to the common good—can be found in sectors of the adult population as well as among the young. But these problems are especially poignant when found among young people, who are in a formative time of life typically characterized by idealism, hopefulness, and elevated ambition. As they search for meaning in their lives, their minds are often open to all possible choices about what to believe, how to live, and what—if anything—to dedicate themselves to. When young people find nothing positive to believe in, they drift in unconstructive and sometimes *de*structive directions. If we take our adult responsibilities seriously, we must try to do everything necessary to see that all of our young people develop the character and competence they need to find purpose in their lives and a positive way to contribute to their society.

In recent years, a vast amount has been written about the inferior standards of academic achievement demonstrated by too many American youth. Not only has this story been widely covered in the press, it also has made its way into the popular cinema, in widely heralded films such as *Waiting for Superman.* The serious gap in academic skills among many of our young people contributes to the problem discussed in this book, and I am pleased that this problem is now receiving the attention of the public. But our academic-skills gap pales in importance to the neglect of character and civic education that we have allowed to develop. As I document, our disregard of civic and moral virtue as an educational priority is having a tangible effect on the attitudes, understanding, and behavior of large portions of the youth population in the United States today.

This is *not* to say that all of our young are languishing. The United States is a large and enormously diverse country. Many young Americans shine with inspiration and purpose, and are acquiring amazing degrees of skill and talent. Others may not be there yet, but are moving in a promising direction that someday will lead them to rewarding and fulfilling commitments. But too many of today's young are floundering or worse: they have no goals that motivate them, and there are no adults in their lives who are providing them with guidance they need to find such goals. I document this situation in later chapters of this book. For now, I simply note that today's cohort of youth is a highly fragmented generation. Popular accounts of a youth generation that can be labeled with a single letter or adjective—X, Y, Z, Millennial, "the dumbest generation," and so on—are little more than fanciful caricatures. The true story of youth today is fragmentation and schism: a younger generation that includes individuals who are on track to becoming sterling citizens but who are growing up next to many others in their cohort who have found nothing to believe in or aspire to and who have little hope of gaining the skills or purpose they will need to succeed and become active citizens.

Today's youth population is so sharply fragmented that many segments seem wholly oblivious to the lives and concerns of all the others. It is astonishing to note that some young Americans are risking their lives fighting in two foreign wars, while the vast majority of their peers shows little interest in anything related to the sacrifices of these devoted youth. Has this level of mutual obliviousness—across an entire generation—occurred ever before in American history? Young Americans have at times dissented from national wars, as during the Vietnam War protests, but at least those protests stood as an indication that those young people (not all of whom were subject to the draft) did care about the state of the nation.

Such a sense of caring is largely missing today—a personal handicap for our young and a looming civic disaster for the nation. As this book will show, we cannot expect our free society to long endure if large portions of its citizenry grow up ill-educated, oblivious to the world and current affairs, out of touch with other members of their generation, and displaying little concern for their responsibilities as American citizens—in short, if they fail to acquire any commitment to civic virtue.

The mission of this book is to expose this very real threat to America's future, a threat far more serious than any foreign enemy could ever pose. It is a danger close at hand, one that has not received 1/100th of the resources that we devote to combating external dangers such as terrorism. Nor has the threat been recognized by our nation's leaders or their policy makers, even though signs of it are everywhere and easy to spot. The most serious danger Americans now face—greater than terrorism—is that our country's future may not end up in the hands of a citizenry capable of sustaining the liberty that has been America's most precious legacy. If present-day trends continue, many young Americans will grow up without an understanding of the benefits, privileges, and duties of citizens in a free society; and without acquiring the habits of character needed to live responsibly in one. As a consequence, many of today's young will be unable to recognize the encroachments on liberty that regularly arise in the normal throes of social life, and too few will be equipped to defend their society against such encroachments.

It is not their fault. It is *we*—today's grown-up generation of parents, educators, opinion leaders, and public officials—who are failing to prepare *them* properly for their futures as citizens in a free society. It is *we* who are failing to fulfill our duty to raise young people for lives of civic virtue. *We* are the ones who are dropping this essential ball, turning our eyes away from a looming loss of national heritage that demands our immediate and concerted attention. Unless we begin to pay attention and meet our challenge as stewards of a priceless heritage, our nation and the future prospects of all individuals dwelling here in years to come will suffer.

This book's message can be summed up in four assertions:

- A free society requires, for its very survival, a citizenry devoted in large part to moral and civic virtue.

- When virtue loses its public footing, too few citizens accept the responsibilities necessary for sustaining liberty in that society.

- In the United States today, we are failing to pass along essential moral and civic virtues to large segments of the youth population.

- Unless we rectify this failure by placing a higher priority on educating young Americans for lives of moral and civic virtue, the nation will move away from liberty and toward despotism—and this movement will be both inevitable and astonishingly quick, perhaps within the space of a generation.

These are not imaginary or hyperbolic warnings. In recent times, most cultural influences on the young have become increasingly less conducive to the cultivation of civic virtue. As I discuss in the first chapter, permissiveness, indulgence, and material inducement have replaced discipline and responsibility as the beacons of child rearing in too many contemporary American homes. Major media influences on today's young commonly emphasize the glittery attractions of celebrity and instant success. The famous figures celebrated in the public limelight are too likely to have chosen vice over virtue as their modes of operation. News stories about substance abuse, sexual scandals, and financial chicanery among the eminent outnumber stories of service, courage, or self-sacrifice by a margin too great to count.

What's more, there is undeniable evidence of vanishing attention to civic and moral virtue among those who make US education policy. At the federal level, education to promote citizenship has become wholly marginalized as a priority over the past decade; promoting character was eliminated as a Department of Education priority in 2009, when the current administration took office. Since federal funding tends to drive local education policies (particularly during hard economic times), this has translated into a severe diminishment of civic and character instruction from school curricula throughout the nation.

Many parents and teachers do not favor this shift in focus, but they are powerless prevent it. The most recent study on the matter, released by American Enterprise Institute (AEI) in September 2010, shows a striking disconnect between those who determine public educational policies and those who raise and teach the young.[1] Funding policies now focus single-mindedly on basic math and literacy skills (with special emphasis on the remedial), squeezing out the time and resources needed to prepare students for citizenship. Yet most teachers and parents believe that citizenship, along with the essential character virtues that it requires, should occupy a central place in American education priorities, as it did in previous periods of US public schooling.[2] Unfortunately, today's federal policies have been winning the day, at least as far as our public schools are concerned, because of the power of federal financial clout. Inattention to this shift by the news media compounds the severity of the loss.

There is no question that this misdirected policy is resulting in deficits in essential civic understanding among students. The AEI report, for example, reveals that no more than 24 percent of social studies teachers (principally responsible for civics instruction in our public schools) are "very confident that most of the students from their high schools have actually learned" a list of core American citizenship concepts; for example, the separation of powers, the protections established by the Bill of Rights, the importance of rules and authority, tolerance for different groups and opinions, and the responsibility to vote and serve on juries.[3] In Chapter 3 of this book, I describe other disturbing dimensions of this deficit, quoting from interviews with contemporary American high school students.

As for the young themselves, as I noted above, the picture is uncomfortably mixed. A significant portion of today's youth population shines with purpose and high aspirations. This is important to acknowledge, because too many accounts of today's young sound as if this entire cohort is destined to be "the dumbest generation," destined to go down the drain together.[4] In our own research at Stanford, we have found at least one-fifth of twelve- to twenty-two-year-olds from varied backgrounds to be reassuringly well directed and very likely on track to becoming capable citizens.[5] But important as that group is, it comprises a relatively small part of the youth population as a whole. For the remaining segments, finding purpose in life is still an elusive aim; and a devotion to moral and civic goals lies at the rear of a long list of personal concerns, if it exists at all. For many young people today, the lures of a celebrity culture and the barrenness of their educational landscape have left little room for broader civic concerns. A distressingly large portion of today's young has found nothing to strive for beyond a day-to-day pursuit of comfort and pleasure.

In this book, I describe living examples of that problem. Although they may be disquieting and even alarming, they will not take many readers by surprise. Anyone living in recent times has witnessed similar examples.

Gratitude and Patriotism

In a study of American civic virtues, gratitude must take a front-and-center place. How can a people blessed with the privileges of American citizenship not feel grateful for the unique rights and opportunities embodied in the American tradition? Or for the sacrifices, efforts, and genius of those who forged that tradition of liberty and democracy?

Yet as I write this, a mood of disaffection—and, in some quarters, strident complaint—is sweeping the country. Gratitude for America's blessings is in short supply. There is no way to know how long this sour mood will last: public opinion in an open democracy can turn around quickly. But for young people raised in the present sociopolitical climate, it is especially hard to find things to believe in or civic leaders to admire. And young people need positive sources of inspiration if they are to become motivated to contribute to the public good.

Isn't it the case, many will argue, that the United States has made grave errors, that the nation's actions nowadays seldom live up to the noble ideals proclaimed in it founding, and that *this* is what young people should be taught for the sake of their critical thinking capacities? Perhaps such statements have some truth to them. But this is far from the whole truth. Critical thinking is worthless unless it is built upon a base of positive concern and caring. To criticize something in order to improve it is an entirely different endeavor than to criticize it in order to detach from it. Young people growing up in the United States need an appreciation for the American tradition to ensure that their critical perspectives on the country will be constructive rather than nihilistic. Any balanced view of American history will conclude that this sense of appreciation is well warranted.

Certainly many shortcomings in the American past have merited complaint, especially for persons and groups that have suffered discrimination and exclusion. But there is a long story of successive liberation and eventual progress in American social life, even if at times too slowly realized. Nor is our story of successive liberation and progress accidental—quite the opposite. The nation was founded with the explicit intention of creating a government that would allow for such progress through reflection and conscious choice. The Founders realized that this would be an uncertain path, at times difficult to forge and always beset by formidable obstacles. Indeed, the Founders predicted that the United States would be a unique and decisive experiment in the ability of humans to enjoy political liberty. *The Federalist* Papers began with this stirring question:

> . . . it seems to have been reserved to the people of this country, by their conduct and example, to decide the important question whether societies of men are really capable or not of establishing good government from reflection and choice, or whether they are forever destined to depend for their political constitutions on accident and force . . . and a wrong election of the part we shall act may, in this view, deserve to be considered as the general misfortune of mankind.[6]

Conceived in this way, as an experiment in good government, individual choice, liberty, and human dignity, the United States occupies a special place in the pantheon of human moral endeavor. However imperfectly, the American tradition has remained true to the intention of the Founders, providing a long string of affirmative answers to their original experimental question. Many of these answers—leading over time to historic gains in expanded liberty for unfairly treated sectors of the society—came in the course of conflict and sacrifice, often fatal. It is neither an overstatement nor a cliché to note that millions of Americans over the centuries have put their lives on the line in the name of freedom.

Concomitant with the "important decision" about governance proclaimed by the authors of *The Federalist* Papers, we must make a personal choice regarding how to feel about our country. If we wish to feel bitter and alienated, there is material to support such a feeling—more, no doubt, for some historical groups than for others. Anyone, of course, has the right to make that choice however one wants and to express it openly; this is one of the cherished privileges of a free society. But there is a highly compelling narrative of liberation and social progress that supports feelings of affection and gratitude for the American tradition. If for nothing else, Americans can feel grateful for the sacrifices and the tangible legacy of political liberty that those who have devoted their lives to the country have provided. As immigrants and observers from all over the world recognize, America still stands as a beacon of hope for people everywhere. This did not happen by itself: many have worked and suffered to make it so.

Gratitude brings with it all kinds of personal and social benefits. It makes possible the positive attitude that enables individuals to seize a moment and take advantage of an opportunity. It generates the devotion that motivates constructive civic participation. Just as importantly, it provides a balancing perspective on civic affairs when events take a wrong turn. Gratitude keeps disappointment from turning sour: the commitment is to work to correct the problem, rather than to disengage and disavow the society that is stumbling.

Similarly, affection brings benefits to both the giver and the receiver. And affection does not imply an uncritical perspective. A parent who loves a child can—and should—call the child to task when he or she has done something wrong. But there is a difference between a parent who loves a child with a critical eye and a parent who disowns a child out of disappointment. This is the difference between a constructive relationship that brings joy to both parties versus a dead end that leads nowhere.

11

The essential civic manifestation of gratitude and affection for one's country is patriotism—the commitment to society that grows out of a spirit of love and appreciation for the benefits that the society has bestowed. The Founders of the United States recognized that love of country and patriotism were inextricably linked to the virtues required to sustain a free society. Thomas Jefferson, for example, copied the following quote from Montesquieu in his *Commonplace Book:*

> In a republic . . . virtue may be defined as the love of the laws and of our country. As such love requires a constant preference of public to private interest, it is the source of all private virtue. . . . Now a government is like everything else: to preserve it we must love it. Everything, therefore, depends on establishing this love in a republic; and to inspire it ought to be the principal business of education, but the surest way of instilling it into children is for parents to set them an example.

In our time (as in other contentious times and places), patriotism has become a contested word. One side of today's political spectrum looks upon it with suspicion and distrust, echoing Samuel Johnson's acerbic witticism that "patriotism is the last refuge of the scoundrel." Too many on the other side claim patriotism as their side's sole property, using it as a political wedge issue and limiting it to token gestures such as waving flags and wearing lapel pins. This is an unhealthy state of affairs for civic cohesion. Debates can and should rage about what are the most sensible and admirable versions of patriotism; but the value of patriotism as a necessary civic virtue should not be doubted. Without a patriotic attachment to one's society, the kinds of full devotion that spur citizens to make crucial sacrifices for the public good could never exist. There are times when every society needs this full devotion for its very survival.

Patriotism, of course, is a *particular* attachment to one's own society. As I discuss in Chapters 3 and 4, some influential educators have objected to fostering patriotism in students because they fear that particular attachments lead inevitably to conflict with those who harbor competing attachments. In the place of patriotism, they would promote "world citizenship" or "cosmopolitanism." In a time of rapid globalization, this argument has found considerable favor among both the intellectual and the business communities— the former wishing to avoid global conflict, the latter wishing to facilitate international commerce.

It is true that particularistic devotions can be exclusionary, discriminatory, and predatory, all of which can create serious moral problems. Moreover, provincialism can be bad for commerce. But patriotism does not need to take a chauvinistic or insular form. It can go hand in hand with a concern for the welfare of people everywhere, with a respect for universal human rights and a belief in universal justice. Indeed, that is exactly in the spirit of the American constitution. The Founders were convinced that the success of their "experiment" would promote human dignity and freedom everywhere—and that its failure would be a "misfortune to all mankind."

Teaching young people to be "citizens of the world" is a popular notion in education today. In fact, the American Enterprise Institute report I cited above found that a majority of US public and private school teachers agree that teaching students "to see themselves as global citizens" is one of twelve core concepts in citizenship education today. Unfortunately, the idea of global citizenship is an empty concept. It contains none of the essential meanings that students need to learn for their own futures as citizens in an actual society: the privileges and rights granted to citizens of a *particular* country, or the duties and obligations to which they are expected to commit themselves. Our students will not be able to vote for a public official of the world; they will not petition to a world court to address a grievance; no global government will project their property or their rights; they will not pay taxes to the world; they will not be inducted to serve in a world jury or in a world army.

Citizenship *is* particularistic. A student can learn how to be a good American citizen only by learning the particular rights and obligations that United States citizenship entails. Students can understand the meaning of these rights and obligations only by learning about the American constitutional tradition as it has evolved since the nation's founding. For American students, patriotism is a particular attachment to this tradition. Based on gratitude and an informed appreciation of the tradition, patriotism gives emotional support to citizenship and serves as the primary source of civic purpose.

Without question, our students need to learn as much as possible about the world beyond our borders. In their work lives, they very likely will participate in the global economy. They should learn about the world's diverse cultures and master foreign languages. As a moral matter, American students should develop an understanding of the perspectives of people around the world, so that they can respond to the needs and problems of others in a humane way. But the present-day emphasis on world citizenship and cosmopolitanism in our schools has been mid-educative for students, because it obscures rather than clarifies what it really means to be a responsible citizen.

The notion of world citizenship works against the very concerns that animate those who promulgate it, such as the fear that patriotism fosters quarrels and injustice. As the philosopher Eamonn Callan has argued, well-directed patriotism has been the strongest weapon in battles against tyranny and injustice, and an important support of freedom and democracy. Callan writes:

> The patriotic sentiment runs deep in many contemporary societies, and in its liberal form it can mitigate against the alienation and ethnic chauvinism that are among the most serious threats to the viability of mass democracy. If the sentiment is somewhat weakened or, worse still, remains strong but comes to be regarded as a bond divorced from the principles of universal justice, our loss may be great. The USA is a revealing case because even though patriotism has commonly been implicated in the worst of American history, it has also had no small role in the best. The struggle against slavery, the Civil Rights movement, and even opposition to the Vietnam War were animated by a commitment to a universal justice. But the commitment was commonly mediated by a love of American democracy and its founding principles. To give up on the task of perpetuating that love from one generation to the next in the name of world citizenship is to forego the moral power of a live tradition for the charms of an imaginative construction.[7]

Patriotism is not the only essential concept that has drawn controversy among educators in recent years. There have been parallels in the handling of indispensible notions such as morality and truth. For an extended period during the latter part of the twentieth century, moral relativism (the belief that there are no universal moral values) became so fashionable that many educators avoided using the term "moral" in their classrooms, believing that the term should be left to fundamentalist groups such as the Moral Majority. At the same time, a smaller (and less influential) contingent was denying the existence of truth on the grounds that perceived reality is inevitably shaped by distorted perspectives, especially perspectives that reflect the self-interests of a "ruling class" that has the power to determine what is presented in cultural settings such as public schools.

Again, as in the case of patriotism, such conclusions are misguided. Arguments about what is morally right and what is true are educative for students; but arguments that there is no such thing as morality or that truth is an illusion make little sense, and they can discourage a student's motivation to learn how best to pursue the good and the true. Fortunately, both intellectual trends may have begun to decline a bit in recent years; and for a broad number of mainstream educators, morality and truth are regaining their status as valued objectives (although, as I discuss in Chapter 2, the way that morality is taught to students still reflects some relativism). It is time for patriotism, the motivational basis for informed and devoted citizenship, to join with morality and truth as the highly valued objectives of education in American schools.

Liberty

The book's title highlights its major concern: as we fail to prepare young people for their rights and responsibilities as American citizens, we fail in our crucial duty to preserve and promote liberty in our society for future generations. In this sense, liberty is the main subject of this book, and its loss will be the most alarming outcome of all the problems I am writing about unless we correct them.

The concept of liberty refers to social and political conditions under which individuals have the right to act according to their own senses of responsibility and personal destiny—to follow the demands and dreams of their own consciences. This is the meaning of liberty that I draw upon in this book.

Liberty in a society makes possible a range of important personal freedoms, including religious, economic, ideological, family, and lifestyle freedoms. But liberty and freedom are not strictly synonymous, because there are some unrestrained freedoms (for example, from individual responsibility, from obligations and duties, and licentiousness) that have the effect of eroding liberty by damaging the social framework needed to protect it. As I argue in this book, it is important to cultivate virtue in young people for the very reason that virtue alone can provide the self-imposed restraints that can enable them to live responsibly under conditions of political liberty. One kind of freedom will play no role in my discussion: the kind referred to in a popular-song lyric of the 1970s—"Freedom's just another word for nothin' left to lose / Freedom ain't worth nothin', but it's free."

For centuries, political philosophers have written about the nature of liberty. As in any scholarly field, debates and distinct ideological positions have been staked out. I am a consumer rather than a maker of political philosophy, and I use a somewhat eclectic mix of these positions in this book. For example, I express concerns about what has been referred to as both "negative" liberty and "positive" liberty:

the former denoting the absence of social interference with private actions; the latter, the capacity to influence the governance of one's society. There have been fascinating debates about whether these two kinds of liberty are compatible, which is primary, and so on.

As interesting as these debates are, they do not constitute the focus of this book. My assumption here is that, for full citizenship, young people must be prepared for both kinds of political liberty: that is, they must learn to live in a free society *and* to participate in its governance. The question I ask is how to prepare them so that they and the generations after them will continue to enjoy access to all the freedoms that political liberty makes possible.

CHAPTER ONE

Youth, Virtue, and the Future of Liberty in American Society

*Only a virtuous people are capable of freedom.
As nations become more corrupt and vicious, they have
more need of masters.* —Benjamin Franklin

The Founders of American democracy clearly saw the importance of a virtuous citizenry. The Founders worried that their bold experiment in human liberty would falter if the American populace chose vice over virtue. Ben Franklin put it this way: "A government can only end in despotism when the people shall become so corrupted as to need despotic government, being incapable of any other." In Franklin's opinion, shared by Jefferson, Washington, Madison, and the philosophers who inspired them (such as John Locke and Edmund Burke), it takes a virtuous citizenry to live responsibly under conditions of liberty. "Among a people generally corrupt," Burke wrote, "liberty cannot long exist." Moreover, for liberty to flourish, it takes a devoted citizenry willing and able to participate in the governing process. What the Founders did not say, but surely implied in their statements about the importance of virtue and personal character, is that such a citizenry must be fashioned by

19

providing its members with a sound upbringing and education during youth.

Modern-day political theorists have recognized the Founders' insights. Peter Berkowitz, for example, has written: "Liberty, as a way of life, is an achievement. This achievement demands of individuals specific virtues . . . certain qualities of mind and character that do not arise spontaneously, but require education and cooperation."[1] Franklin's concern that self-governance could be lost from neglect also has appeared in the writings of social commentators for much of the modern era. The great twentieth-century scholarly leader Robert Maynard Hutchins once wrote that "The death of democracy is not likely to be an assassination from ambush. It will be a slow extinction from apathy, indifference and undernourishment."

But despite such clarion warnings, the conditions necessary for sustaining a free society are not well understood in today's popular culture. Liberty is understood to signify the freedom to pursue self-centered desires without restriction—and this stunted conception is reflected in many young Americans' notions about their privileges, rights, and obligations as citizens. Many young people have never been taught anything else. Such misunderstandings by adults are passed along to the children; and the vestiges of understanding that do remain are lost in translation on their way through a leaky educational system.

Regarding popular understandings of liberty in today's society, the philosopher Jacob Needleman has written:

> At the root of the American ideal of liberty is the right of every human being to search for and attend to the dictates of conscience. Political liberty means first and foremost the

social conditions necessary to allow this search. . . . But this ideal and right has been taken to mean merely the right to satisfy one's own subjective desires, whatever they may be, without any reference to the existence of the moral law within. In this way, the idea of liberty descends into the glorification of desire as such, which is an infantilization of its fundamental meaning.[2]

A society that allows its young to learn nothing more than an infantilized version of that society's core ethic is placing itself at risk for eventual dissolution. We must do better, both for the well-being of the young and for the preservation of American liberty. We cannot abandon young Americans to a state of permanent moral and political infancy.

But first, to open the case that I present in this book, let us give infancy its due. I begin with an examination of the building blocks of character—the moral virtues that are present in every child at birth or shortly thereafter.

The Development of Virtue and Moral Character

In the human species, the seeds of virtue are present as early as infancy. Moral-response systems—such as outrage, self-regulation, empathy, and shame—can be observed at birth or shortly thereafter in every normal child.[3] They provide a strong natural basis for virtue and moral character.

But this does not mean that the full development of virtuous character is assured for all individuals in society. Initially, the budding moral-response systems consist only of transient inclinations or aversions, and these rudimentary leanings alone cannot in themselves provide a sufficient basis for a virtuous life. In order to grow into stable moral commitments, these premature leanings must be informed and strengthened through education.

Education for virtue can take place in homes, schools, and common settings such as workplaces, sports teams, and religious institutions (and ideally across several of these settings in conjunction with one another[4]). A number of combinations will work; but the education must take place *somewhere* if the child is to grow into a responsible member of society. Without an education that teaches clear moral standards, the child's natural virtues will atrophy over time, and the formation of the child's moral character will be placed at risk.

At present, the state of virtue among young Americans, according to prominent indicators of youth conduct, is a decidedly mixed bag. Rates of antisocial and destructive behaviors among the young have declined over the past twenty years, but this has been a decline from a very high base rate.[5] The variability of youth behavior in present-day American society is enormous. Some young people are acting as shining examples of decency and devotion, while others are leading directionless or dissolute lives. Most disturbingly, recent studies have shown that only a minority of the young has found any moral or civic purpose to which they wish to dedicate themselves; and many express little interest in any cause beyond their own gratification.[6] In particular, civic purpose—an interest in social policy, learning about current events and political matters, aspiring to positions of community leadership, taking citizenship responsibilities such as voting in elections seriously—comes in last among the life goals held by the present cohort of young Americans.[7] While virtue and purpose are alive and well for many members of our younger generation, many others seem stalled on their path to mature character development. Only a small minority (in recent studies, no more than one in five) shows strong signs of making solid progress toward assuming roles as responsible citizens in our society.[8] This shaky situation is no accident. All of the institutions that I mentioned above—homes, schools, and community organizations of work, faith, and recreation—have come up short in their obligations to educate the young for lives of virtue. The reasons are multiple: they include a mix of unresponsive educational practices, uninformed social policies, irresponsible mass media, community disintegration, waning traditional belief systems, the dubious values of post-modern culture, and legions of homes bereft of constructive guidance. I will expound on these contributing causes in subsequent chapters of this book. For now, suffice it to say that the goal of a supportive character education for all young people has diminished as a priority in virtually every setting where they spend their time in American society.

There are, of course, some exceptions; but these are becoming increasingly rare and at odds with contemporary sensibilities. The idea that the education of the young should focus on virtue seems old fashioned, beside the point, and time wasting to many professional educators today.

In response to this dismissal of virtue as a marginal concern left over from bygone days, I raise in this book an urgent question of national interest for a country that long has stood as a bastion of human liberty. The question is whether our democracy, and the freedoms that it makes possible, can flourish in the future if we cannot manage to cultivate moral and civic virtue in a more extensive portion of our younger generation. My answer to this question,

23

which I explicate in this book, is that I do not believe that any society that fails to develop moral character and civic purpose in its young has much future as a land of freedom and democracy. Cultivating virtue in our young is every bit as vital to preserving freedom in our society as is military strength—although it is certainly less newsworthy and less politically evocative.

The Essential Personal and Moral Virtues

Lists of essential human virtues date back at least to Aristotle, and generally such lists include both personal and moral strengths. Aristotle, for example, included courage, which is neutral in its moral significance (it can be employed for both pro- and antisocial causes), along with more benevolent qualities such as generosity, friendship, and truthfulness. The mix of personal and moral in Aristotle's accounting is consistent with the original etymological root of the term "virtue," which literally meant "strength" in the ancient Greek language. "Character" has long been considered to be the sum of a person's acquired virtues.

Contemporary psychological science has followed a similar approach in including both personal and moral strengths under the rubric of virtue. In a recent initiative, the burgeoning "positive psychology" movement has produced a catalogue of twenty-four virtues considered necessary for "authentic happiness."[9] Among these "happiness" virtues are *strengths of wisdom*, such as creativity, intelligence, and love of learning; *strengths of courage*, such as bravery and zest; *strengths of humanity*, such as kindness and compassion; *strengths of justice*, such as fairness and cooperation; *strengths of temperance*, such as prudence, mercy, forbearance, and self-regulation; and *strengths of transcendence*, such as gratitude, hope, and faith. This highly inclusive list is intended to serve as a comprehensive set of the basic psychological strengths that can be measured, fostered, and repaired by therapy ("coaching," in positive psychology's new lexicon), should such treatment be called for.

But some scholars (myself included), prefer to reserve the term "virtue" only for the types of behavior intended to produce social good. When used in this way, the term has an inevitable moral connotation. All the studies in moral and "character" education that I refer to in this book employ the term in this way.[10] In the body of work from moral psychology, virtues are considered to be enduring habits of good behavior that enable people to lead lives of integrity, responsibility, compassion, and honor. Such virtues may well lead to personal happiness, but that is not their defining feature: rather, the claim to "virtuousness" rests on a dedication to the social and moral good.

When writing or speaking of the kind of virtue they deemed necessary for life in a free society, the Founders of American democracy unquestionably had the social and moral good firmly in mind. In the views of Ben Franklin, George Washington, and other Founders, the good life required self-improvement—a striving toward "moral perfection" (Franklin's phrase) through the pursuit of virtue. The "pursuit of happiness" was also cited—famously—as a legitimate goal; but it is clear that the meaning of the term "happiness" during that period focused on being free to follow one's conscience and find one's God, rather than on achieving the kinds of hedonistic and materialistic rewards that have been associated with happiness in modern times.[11]

25

Ben Franklin was specific about the virtues he believed were required for moral perfection: Temperance; Silence (known today as discretion); Order; Resolution (what we might call dedication or commitment); Frugality (or thrift); Industry (now termed the work ethic); Sincerity (honesty); Justice (including what we now call empathy); Moderation; Cleanliness; Tranquility (now known as emotional balance); Chastity; and Humility. Given Franklin's unique accomplishments and insights into the workings of political liberty, his list of virtues should be taken seriously by anyone concerned with the qualities necessary for a citizenry to sustain a free society. Naturally, the list reflects Franklin's personal experiences as a successful businessman and diplomat as well as his interests in social reformation. It is a collection of virtues that, if widely acquired, would make for a fair-minded, well-mannered, tolerant, and amiable citizenry. As philosopher Harvey Mansfield has commented, "Franklin's list of virtues for a free society . . . might be summed up as sociability under an aura of modesty."[12]

It is informative to examine Franklin's virtues in light of the extensive research on moral development that has been conducted in the social and psychological sciences over the centuries since he made his list. In recent years, much of this research has been driven by neurologically based efforts to locate the seat of human morality in sectors of the brain and by genetically based efforts to demonstrate that certain moral dispositions are native to the species and thus inherited. As I mentioned at the start of the chapter, showing that morality has a physiological and genetic base does not mean that character can be acquired without significant social influence. Each virtue that Franklin identifies requires both a well-directed education and sustained personal effort in order to develop into part of a fully formed moral character. And some virtues require more education and effort than others.

Some of Franklin's virtues (the ones he called Temperance, Order, Justice/empathy, and Moderation) have roots in highly evolved behavioral dispositions that are native to our species. Modern social science has named these "natural virtues" self-control, obligation, empathy, and fairness.[13] Studies of newborns and infants using sophisticated video scanning techniques have identified behavioral precursors to each of these virtues in virtually all children born without severe brain damage. Yet these native dispositions lack social effectiveness and continuity: they require elaboration and reinforcement over the course of development if they are to not to atrophy; and they require constant practice and learning if they are to guide moral action in useful and dependable ways throughout life.

Take empathy (a significant component of Franklin's Justice) as an example. As the emotional foundation of what will later become genuine compassion, empathy can be first observed in the cries of an infant who observes another person in distress. But this instinctive response comes with no plan of action or prescription for whom to empathize with; and the responder is easily distracted. In children with backgrounds of violence and abuse, the empathic response can grow into a grotesque caricature of itself. For example, a therapist working with delinquent youth groups recorded one homicidal youngster saying that he felt brokenhearted whenever he thought about people cutting down trees for Christmas.[14] This boy had wreaked violence on numerous people without regret, yet he experienced vestiges of empathic sadness for fallen pine

27

trees. The annals of criminal justice are full of such cases: psychopaths who have empathic feelings for an animal or a little sister but who treat virtually everyone else with absolute callousness.

Like all the natural virtues, empathy in its mature form draws upon guidance and experience. The family in particular is the prime setting for the cultivation of the natural virtues of empathy, self-control, and obligation.[15] The cultivation of fairness often occurs in the peer settings of play and friendship.[16] In each of these cases, thanks to the biological dispositions of our species, the child has inherited a head start in developing the virtue. It takes the right kinds of social influences—family, peer, education, experience—plus a good deal of practice and learning to turn these natural dispositions into true virtues. But the foundations are there at birth.

Other virtues on Franklin's list (such as Industry, Frugality, Sincerity, Chastity, and Cleanliness) are more cultural, requiring a greater degree of explicit instruction and training. Industry, for example, is a virtue that is more honored in some cultural settings than others, as studies of the work ethic throughout history have shown.[17] To date, none of the culturally driven virtues on Franklin's list has been shown to have biological roots.

As agents of culture, families, peers, and the community can foster the acquisition of the culturally driven virtues. In addition, schools, at least when they are operating well, also can play consequential roles. Industry, for example, can be engendered through family practices such as household chores, reinforced in school by regular homework assignments, and encouraged by adults and peers in the community who honor and respect the work ethic.

The implications of the scientific research on the acquisition of virtue are clear. In cases where virtue has strong *genetic* foundations, training and experience are required to turn the inherited early-response systems into effective and reliable moral habits. In cases where the foundations are *cultural*, instruction and practice are required to convey the importance of the virtue to the growing child. In both cases, responsible adults—in homes, schools, and the community—need to provide guidance. Laissez-faire approaches to children's development cannot ensure the transmission of essential virtues across the generations. People are not born with fully formed moral character. Virtues, the elements of moral character, cannot mature by themselves in a cultural vacuum.

Today, in twenty-first-century America, our problem lies more in combating the *reality* of laissez-faire approaches to children's education than in contesting the *philosophy* of the romantic idea that children are born with all the natural goodness they will need to live an upstanding moral life. This is something of a change from the recent past, though it is not enough of an improvement to make a conspicuous difference. During the latter half of the twentieth century, educators and childrearing experts became enamored of the romantic view that celebrates children's autonomy and disparages discipline and authority of any kind.[18] In a manner reminiscent of Rousseau, the fashionable philosophy was to treat them as equals and allow them to "flower," avoiding such constraints on their creativity and natural goodness as discipline, challenges, or service responsibilities. While vestiges of this approach still persist in many homes and schools, as a cultural trend it has (in many places) been replaced by a vigorous standards movement and a stronger ethic of achievement and service.[19] The desultory results of permissiveness, low expectations, and excessively child-centered practices became too obvious for much of the general public to ignore by the end of the last century.

Yet, in practice, our society has not gotten past laissez-faireism in the way it raises and educates many of today's young. Because of current ill-conceived social and educational policies, we have become unable to provide the guidance necessary to ensure that the essential virtues are acquired in large segments of the younger generation. Although some young people are fortunate to grow up in situations where they are able to receive such guidance, there are gaping holes in our society's networks of youth guidance, and unacceptably large numbers of youth are falling through these holes.

Families without at least a modicum of stability and continuity cannot establish the household routines that provide children with opportunities to learn virtues such as industry, self-control, and obligation. Families without the presence of dependable adults cannot provide children with examples of virtue they can emulate, nor can they offer the regular occasions needed to explain the nature and importance of virtuous behavior in the often-confusing social world that the child is entering.

Yet, in our present society, the state of the family is deteriorating. Increasing numbers of children do not even start with an intact family. In the period from 1960 to 2005 (the most recent year for which data are available), the percentage of births to unmarried women has increased from 5.3 percent to 36.8 percent—a *sevenfold* increase.[20] These days, over a quarter of births to woman ages 25 to 29, and over half to woman ages 20 to 24, occur out of wedlock. For the children who are born into an intact family, the odds that their parents will stay together are lower in American society than in any other industrial nation. Divorce, short-term co-habitation, and single parenthood are common patterns in families today. A 2010 report entitled *When marriage disappears*, produced by the online marital-research project http://stateofourunions.org, begins with the comment "In middle America, marriage is in trouble." The report shows how all but the most educated and affluent Americans have turned away from stable marriage as a goal in life, to the detriment of their own social well-being and that of their children. As the sociologist Andrew Cherlin has documented in a recent study, Americans now "step on and off the carousel of intimate relationships" with astonishing frequency.[21]

It is not hard to see how family instability can leave children without a sufficient structure of guidance at the most formative period in their character development. Indeed, Cherlin and others have found family instability to be linked to higher rates of pregnancy, substance abuse, truancy, criminality, and behavioral problems in school.[22] Nonetheless, the policy response to the destabilization of American families has been minimal at best. Beyond occasional verbal injunctions from our political leaders, family solidarity has received no meaningful economic or legal support—indeed, just the opposite in many ways, since our tax laws penalize marriage, and divorce laws encourage separation and litigation rather than persistence and reconciliation in marriages.

Even where it still exists, family stability alone cannot be the entire answer for providing children with the guidance they need to develop virtue in today's world. All of today's families are surrounded by a mass culture that has become increasingly unsavory over the past half century.

The graphic quality and extent of the violent and sexualized images in the entertainment media marketed to young people today would have been unfathomable a few decades ago. This is not just a problem of greater access to trashy content through the underground media or the Internet. The elite bastions of our culture now applaud the most unwholesome elements in youth entertainment, perhaps from the standpoint that you can't argue with success. A laudatory 2009 article in *The New Yorker*, on a filmmaker whom "teenagers around the world have turned into a celebrity," describes with relish a scene in which "a woman shaves her legs in the bathtub and discovers that she's actually shaving off her skin;" and the piece concludes admiringly with this quote from the filmmaker: "I'm ready to start chopping up body parts again."[23]

The adverse influences of the entertainment media run even deeper than the ghoulishness of the images that are marketed for shock and titillation purposes. The real damage is done by a warped view of interpersonal relationships, work, and civic society that is broadcast daily to young people throughout our society. Media studies reveal a pattern of cynicism, disparagement, and contempt for traditional ideals that permeates most of today's youth entertainment.[24]

In the sitcom view of family life, parents (and especially fathers) are clueless fools in constant need of correction by the kids. Business leaders are shown as greedy and predatory (not to mention their constant alcoholism, infidelity, and other vices); and public officials generally come off as corrupt and/or incompetent. Perhaps the most misleading of the spectacles produced by today's entertainment industry are the so-called reality and instant-celebrity TV shows, which send viewers the message that success is a matter of

winning sudden fame and fortune through showy perfor-
mances. The fact that personal advancement almost always
comes as a reward for genuine accomplishment, persistence,
hard work, and service, rather than as a prize for glittering
displays of rapid bravado, rarely makes its way into these
widely viewed shows. In the culture of our popular media
today, celebrity has replaced the work ethic.

Similarly, much of the media fare consumed by young
people today slights the importance of individual responsibility as a determining factor in human affairs. Media studies have documented the increased theme of victimhood as
an explanation for social and personal causality in recent
pop-culture presentations.[25] The notion that the major forces
determining human destiny are beyond an individual's
reach has long contrasted with the traditional American
view that individuals can take charge of their own lives and
their own society. It also is a significantly less hopeful view
of human resilience than the up-by-your-bootstraps vision
promoted by the American popular literature of earlier
eras. As social critics have noted, encouraging citizens—
especially younger ones—to identify themselves as helpless
victims of circumstance amounts to a prescription for fostering the character types that accept the dictates of a despotic
society.[26] In contrast, a belief in individual control among
young people fosters hope and purpose, setting the stage for
engaged democratic citizenship. Unfortunately, a belief in
individual determination is not common nowadays.

In today's cultural environment, families need do more
than stay intact within their own boundaries. They must
also help their children navigate the wilderness of influences that children will encounter in the world outside the
home. Yet how many families are prepared to provide their

children with informed feedback on such influences or to take steps to counteract the effects of an irresponsible but immensely powerful mass media? What about our schools? Are they doing their part in educating students for virtue—in particular the culturally driven virtues that rely heavily on explicit instruction and training? By and large, with the exception of some token efforts at character education, most public schools have taken themselves out of the virtue-building business. This is a dramatic change from the early days of public schooling in America, when almost every reader and textbook included prescriptions about how to lead a moral life.[27] Until well into the twentieth century, schools were expected to foster both academic and moral learning.

All this has changed in the post-modern era. Academic learning has come to dominate character as public schooling's clear priority, and schools have become places where children are sent solely to learn knowledge and skills. At the present time, in an era that focuses on the most basic skills of numeracy and literacy, the moral agenda appears as little more than a distraction from the hard and urgent task of raising test scores. Classroom time is seen as too precious to spend on "non-academic" matters such as acquiring virtue or helping the child acquire a moral compass to guide the skills the school has taught.

In addition to choices about what to spend their time teaching—or not teaching—schools have a way of influencing their students' development that can be more potent than actual instructional agendas. This is often known as the "hidden curriculum," which derives from the atmosphere that a school creates as it conducts its business. A school that operates in an orderly, fair, and sincere manner evokes trust from its students. In turn, the students in such a school will respect the authority of the school and learn the virtues it embodies.

This is far from the situation in many public schools today. The worst of our schools are disorderly, graffiti-ridden, and in disrepair. In such places, virtually everyone is demoralized. But even in our better-tended schools, the hidden curriculum is in many cases awry. Because of legalistic challenges on behalf of student rights, teachers have become hesitant to exercise any moral authority on issues as central to education as honesty and academic integrity.[28]

Cheating is rife in almost every school, with 86 percent of high school students, according to one study, admitting that they would readily cheat on their tests if they could get away with it.[29] Grades are inflated to the point of meaninglessness—again, often due to a fear of legal challenges—and homework assignments are loosely enforced at best or, in many cases, entirely lacking. The work that does get assigned is bereft of anything approaching inspiration. Little wonder that virtues such as diligence, purpose, and devotion are in short supply among many of today's student populations.

Adding to the diminished moral authority and low academic standards of public schooling nowadays is the overall climate of moral relativism that influenced the intellectual currents of our time, an anything-goes ethic that makes no distinctions between right and wrong, and that validates no standards outside the individual's own, subjective sentiments. As one might expect, the versions of this ethic that trickle down into public school classrooms tend to be less nuanced and less charming than those one encounters in post-modern literary journals. But the audiences for today's schoolhouse relativism are students who are still forming their attitudes about the kinds of people they want to become; and the effects of such messages rarely come down on the side of virtue.

Chester Finn, president of the Thomas B. Fordham Foundation for Advancing Educational Excellence, has written the following regarding the moral climate of today's public schools.

> The regular public schools . . . have become more secular . . . and more value-free. The education profession's cherished "progressivism" is part of the reason. And the close scrutiny of fierce watchdog groups . . . has made schools and educators gun-shy. In recent years, however, perhaps the strongest influences have been postmodern relativism and multiculturalism, which first trickled, then gushed from university campuses into primary and secondary school classrooms. If scholars, teachers, and those who train them abjure fixed distinctions between right and wrong, if all judgments are said to depend upon one's unique perspective or background rather than universal standards of truth, beauty, or virtue, if every form of family, society, and polity is deemed equal to all other forms, and if every group's mores and values must be taught . . . who is there (in school) to help children determine what it means to be an American, how to behave, and what to believe?[30]

The following chapter will take up the problem of how today's public schools are failing to educate students for virtue. In later chapters of the book, I will also examine the other urgent issue that Finn introduces at the close of the comment above: what does it mean for a young person today to be an American? Subsumed in this general question are related questions about civic virtue and citizenship: for example, what responsibilities do young Americans have as emerging members of a democratic society; and what essential features of the American tradition deserve to be appreciated and protected by its citizens?

If the American way of life, with all its freedoms, privileges, and opportunities, is to be preserved for future generations, such questions must be understood and addressed by the young people of today. But at this time, too few public schools are doing their part in fostering either appreciation or understanding of these questions among their students. Among the confused welter of short-sighted priorities and reflexive ideological biases, such essential matters are not addressed often enough in our schools today.

CHAPTER TWO

The Virtues Gap in Education Today

The first duty of every adult is to teach children
to find pleasure in the right things.   —Plato

During the years when children are learning the habits and values that will shape their behavioral choices in life, they spend about thirty hours a week in schooling of one kind or another—public, private, charter, parochial, or home. For ten months a year from ages five to eighteen, school consumes the lion's share of most children's waking time and attention. Much of their social lives revolve around their schools, and in no place other than home do they receive more attention or more information about how to live. As a consequence, for better or for worse, schools are one of the major formative influences on the character development of most American youth.

Some have argued that virtue cannot be sufficiently taught through explicit school instruction. This is true in a strict sense, in that children need more than verbal lessons to acquire good character; and yet explicit school instruction certainly can have an influence on a child's values, judgment, and conduct. Moreover, beyond explicit instruction, the implicit rules, expectations, messages, role models, and social conventions that students encounter unquestionably affect their character and conduct. In school, students learn about how to act in a real-life society with responsibilities, roles, and relationships. Because schools impart both direct and indirect influence, schooling inevitably shapes moral development and—when conducted properly—trains students for lives of virtue. If virtue is to be widely cultivated among the young in twenty-first-century America, it will be necessary for schools of every sort to play a positive and constructive role.

But What About the Family's Role?

Traditionally, of course, the family has been considered to be a main seed bed of virtue for members of the younger generation; and it remains the first and foremost influence on many children's character development. But as I mentioned in the previous chapter, the days when the family as a social institution could be counted upon to instill character in a major portion of the nation's young are long past. Although it will always remain highly beneficial for parents to pass along strong moral values to their own children, it has become unrealistic to imagine that the institution of the family alone can produce a virtuous citizenry for the United States as a whole.

One reason for this is that children are spending increasing amounts of time away from their homes, pursuing expanding interests in peer, school, work, and entertainment settings. What's more, even when at home, children are exposed to a vast and practically uncontrollable variety of influences through their communications devices, television, the Internet, audio and video programming, and other mass media sources. These days, even the most attentive parents are inevitably only one among several parts of the child-rearing picture. What's more, many parents are not as attentive as they might wish to be because of economic, health, or other pressures on their own lives.

Another reason for the limited capacity of today's families to raise and socialize America's children is that the idea of committing to families of their own has lost appeal for many adults of marrying age. The average age of marriage in the United States (and in other industrial countries such as Japan and Italy) has risen by several years over the past generation, and the overall rate of marriage among adults has dwindled significantly in recent times. The percentage of married adults in the United States has declined from 76 percent in 1970 to under 60 percent today. (The all-time low point was actually reached just as this book went to press: only 52 percent of Americans aged 18 and over are now married.) Related to this trend, the percentage of children born to married parents has declined, in little more than a generation, by a startling one-third—from 89 percent to 60 percent.[1]

For many people today, marriage is perceived as an arbitrary and unnecessary social arrangement. An October 2010 Pew Research Center survey reported that almost two of five Americans now believe that marriage is becoming obsolete. A similar survey in 1978 found only slightly more than one-quarter expressing this sentiment.

Marriage, of course, is not synonymous with family. There are many nonmarital types of families, including those with children raised by widowed and separated parents; and it is certainly the case that a child raised in a nonmarital family can do just as well as any other child. But studies have found that, for many families, these nonmarital patterns are not as stable as marriage.[2] Research also has established that children raised in intact, two-parent families tend to be more closely supervised and less prone to behavioral problems than children from nonintact families.[3] It does not signal disrespect for dedicated nonmarried people who raise children—nor should it convey any negative stigmata for children raised in nonmarried families—to point out that stable marriage is the most time-tested human context for rearing the young in a manner benefiting them and their society. The fading status of marriage is without question implicated in the diminishing degree to which today's children are likely to receive the benefits of a two-parent family.

The decline in the American family may be troubling, but it is stubbornly hard to change. The multitudes of experts who point to the benefits of intact family life have little power to reverse the social and economic forces that have made it difficult for families to form or stay together. It may be possible that, at some point in the unforeseeable future, the widely shared conclusions of social scientists could translate into policies that could reinvigorate the American family and provide support to parents who find it necessary to raise children without a partner. But even the most wide-eyed optimists would be hard pressed to predict the implementation of such policies any time soon or to imagine a world in which the broad majority of American children would be raised in families that have the resources, know-how, and determination to provide in their own homes all the guidance and supervision that today's children need for their character development.

The Inescapable
Responsibility of Schools Today

The decline in family control and stability has created a vacuum that other institutions that care for children must now fill. All of our institutions—religious, athletic, vocational, recreational, civic, and community—can and should make efforts to accomplish this essential mission. Many voluntary organizations, such as the Boy Scouts and Girl Scouts, have played highly positive roles in the character development of young people. But the single institution that must take responsibility for all children in our society is the school.

It is the school alone that can reach children from every background and every type of family, whether well functioning or not. Schooling affords an opportunity to educate every child for a life of purpose and virtue. It is crucial to make the best use of this opportunity, not just for the sake of the lives of the children who need more of an education than they can receive in their homes, but also for the preservation of a free society that depends upon responsible citizens. Our schools have both a moral and civic responsibility to cultivate virtue in our younger generation.

In order to accomplish this mission, schools must begin by exemplifying virtue in the way they themselves conduct their everyday affairs. There is a hidden curriculum of schooling that has more of a direct effect on students' values and conduct than any lesson plan. This curriculum consists of the school's social order, the way in which rules are either enforced or not enforced, the kinds of expectations that students encounter, the ways in which such expectations are communicated and modeled by the teachers and staff, the modes of evaluation and discipline employed, and the manner in which teachers deal with students.[4]

The Promotion of Virtue in the Hidden Curriculum: an Endangered Practice

Gradually over the past fifty years, public schools have stepped away from the hidden curriculum of values they once offered to students by enforcing the standards of honesty, fairness, civility, moral authority, and social order within their own academic settings. Going to school traditionally has meant conforming to its rules and respecting the authority of the teacher. But during the past five decades, litigation and legal judgments on behalf of "student rights" have reduced the likelihood that students will adopt a respectful orientation to school authority. Many school rules are no longer seen as fair by students, and teachers hesitate to take stands that assert moral authority—stands they believe could expose them to lawsuits. This is even the case with regard to issues involving academic integrity, such as cheating and honest grading, issues that in fact go beyond any actual legal ruling.

As a result, today's students have been shut off from the moral guidance of an important group of adults in their lives—the teachers and staff who supervise their everyday school activities. Combined with a school curriculum that has been stripped of much of its moral content (as I discuss later in this chapter), this litigation-induced decline in school authority has seriously diminished the capacity of public schools to cultivate virtue in America's young.

A classic technique for fostering virtuous behavior in children is the judicious use of discipline. In the past, school disciplinary practices included mild corporal punishment (such as the iconic slap of the teacher's ruler on the knuckles), isolation (standing in the corner facing the wall), suspension, expulsion, extra work, and negative report cards. Corporal punishment is now prohibited—wisely so, since methods such as withholding privileges and providing negative reports and other penalties are safer and more effective. But less wisely, other disciplinary methods have also come under attack in the litigious climate of today's society.

Richard Arum, a professor at New York University, has demonstrated how legal attacks in the name of student rights have undermined the capacity of public schools to discipline students. Arum has shown how this has led to a radical departure from the public school's crucial role in educating students for virtue by exercising moral authority: "Until the late 1960's," he writes, "parents and students rarely challenged the disciplinary actions of school authorities, viewing common schools as providing instruction, instilling virtue, and fostering the ideals of our nation."[5] All this has changed, destabilizing the moral atmosphere required for a school to cultivate responsibility and respect in its students.

Arum and his colleagues have documented the surge in litigation over student rights since the 1960s.[6] A landmark US Supreme Court case in 1975 (*Goss v. Lopez*) granted students due process rights whenever they were suspended. This precedent-setting decision was followed by a host of local and appellate court cases aimed at challenging the authority of schools to discipline and evaluate their students. Since 1993, Arum finds, the number of such cases has escalated sharply, sending a loud message to students and teachers that a lawsuit awaits anyone who doles out a disciplinary response to a student's misbehavior. As a consequence, many teachers have learned to look the other way; and many students have learned to disrespect their school's authority.

Ironically, the message sent by the widely publicized legal cases is more strident than the actual case law warrants. For example, no rulings have established that students are entitled to legal due process when they are unhappy with their grades or even when they have been given poor grades for disciplinary reasons; yet as many as a third of students believe this to be the case.[7] Teachers harbor similar misconceptions and often limit their feedback to students accordingly. Not surprisingly, this expansive perception of student entitlements has directly affected student attitudes toward school discipline. Arum and his colleagues report a significant correlation between the extent to which students believe they have a legal entitlement to sue their school and the extent to which they consider the rules of the school unfair.[8]

In response to the threat of such lawsuits, schools have felt forced to institute increasingly formal and rigid procedures that cannot be challenged in court because they allow for no discretion or flexibility in the way they are administered. For example, many schools, in order to avoid ambiguities, have adopted "zero tolerance" policies leading directly to extreme measures such as suspension. Students naturally consider such policies to be harsh and unfair. Hence the spawning of a counterproductive cycle: students' disrespect fosters an increasingly authoritarian response on the part of the school, which then results in an intensification of the students' sense of unfairness.

The results of this unhappy development? Studies by Arum and his colleagues find that "students who perceive school discipline as unfair are more likely to disobey teachers, disrupt classroom instruction, and in general fail to develop behaviors conducive to educational success. . . ." Overall, he concludes, "schools have moved away from disciplinary practices that rely on the judgment, discretion, and actions of professional educators and have turned instead . . . to techniques that are ill suited to the pedagogical task of enhancing the moral authority of educators to support the socialization of youth, that is, the internalization of norms, values, and rules."[9]

The value of discipline in socializing the young is that it sends a message: we care enough about these rules and standards that we will take pains to enforce them by responding to any breeches with consequences. Such consequences make the message harder to ignore than if the message were delivered merely by lesson or lecture. In order for the message to be taken seriously, the discipline must be reliable, consistent, and not unreasonable. If the consequences are enforced only arbitrarily and sporadically, or if the punishment poorly fits the crime (by either being too mild or too extreme), the message will lose its legitimacy and hence its power to influence behavior.

The benefits of consistent disciplinary practices have long been established in studies of socialization.[10] They also have been clearly demonstrated in the outcomes of social policy initiatives in the criminal-justice arena. For example, a "broken windows" approach to crime, adopted in the 1990s by New York City mayor Rudolph Guiliani and police chief

William Bratton, reduced criminal behavior by consistently pursuing perpetrators of common minor violations of the law, such as vandalism and disorderly conduct. The punishments were predictable and appropriately gauged, sending the message that the law is reliable, rational, and just. When such a message is learned at an early age, it contributes powerfully to the virtue of self-control.[11]

Cheating

Every school is a microcosm of society, with a full range of relationships that must be respected and rules that must be followed if chaos is not to ensue. All the rules and relationships provide learning opportunities for students, most of whom who have not yet developed a full understanding of their social and moral responsibilities. Just as in the wider world, students must learn to respect the order within their schools in order to benefit from the privileges they are given. Even a routine gesture such as walking quietly in the corridors trains a student in the virtuous habit of respectfulness.

All the rules are important. But some get especially close to the heart of what the academic mission is all about. Foremost among these are codes of academic integrity. Of all the moral breeches that can tear deeply into the moral fabric of a school, cheating may be among the most damaging, throwing into doubt the school's allegiance to truth and fairness. In a moral sense, cheating in school is wrong for (at least) four reasons: 1) it gives students who cheat an unfair advantage over those who do not; 2) it is an act of dishonesty in a context defined by a quest for truthful knowledge; 3) it violates the trust between student and teacher;

and 4) it disrespects the code of conduct and the social order of the school.

One would therefore expect that cheating would provide educators with an ideal platform for imparting the key moral standards of honesty, integrity, trust, and fairness. Certainly everyday conduct in schools provides opportunities aplenty: research has shown that over three-quarters of American *college* students admit to having cheated at least once in their high school academic work.[12]

Yet responses to cheating in our schools today are haphazard at best. Many teachers, in order to avoid legal contention and other possible conflicts, look the other way if their students copy exam answers or hand in plagiarized papers. Some teachers sympathize with student cheaters because tests are flawed or unfair.[13] Some excuse students because they believe that sharing schoolwork is motivated by loyalty to friends. Incredibly, some even encourage their students to cheat, or actually cheat themselves in reporting student test scores. In a recent feature on New York State academic testing, CBS News reported the following: "New York education officials found 21 proven cases of teacher cheating. Teachers have read off answers during a test, sent students back to correct wrong answers, photocopied secure tests for use in class, inflated scores, and peeked at questions, then drilled those topics in class before the test."[14]

Such blatant infractions are, hopefully, the exception rather than the rule. Still, for the most part, school programs regarding academic integrity and cheating consist of little more than a patchwork of vaguely stated prohibitions and ad-hoc responses.[15] Many schools vacillate wildly between neglect and hysterical overreaction if the problem boils over into a public media scandal. There is little consistency, coherence, or transparency in public school cheating policies; and it is practically impossible to find a school that treats academic integrity as a moral issue, using exposed incidents of cheating to communicate to its student body values such as honesty, respect for rules, and trust.

The result of this failure in moral response is an unmitigated decline in students' moral and behavioral standards. Donald McCabe, the most prominent contemporary researcher on this subject, has concluded that in our time, "Cheating is prevalent, and . . . some forms of cheating have increased dramatically in the last 30 years."[16] This dreary consequence is hardly surprising. In my own experience, when I have been invited into schools to resolve cheating scandals, I have found a palpable resistance among teachers and staff to the idea of discussing the moral significance of the breech with students.[17] This is one sign among many that moral language may be the scarcest commodity of all in US public schooling these days.

Our Missing Moral Language

A moral language is a language of right and wrong. It conveys judgments about widely accepted standards of personal responsibility for the common good. I do not refer here to arbitrary linguistic distinctions that have arisen through historical accident; nor to customs and conventions that reflect some supposed agenda of the ruling classes, as postmodernists have claimed. Rather, I refer to a language that expresses the essential norms of social behavior: honesty, fairness, compassion, common decency, respect for the rights of others and for legitimate authority. As in any civilized society, the micro-society of the school cannot exist, let alone flourish, in the absence of such norms.

Yet in our current approach to schooling, the use of a moral language has become a matter of controversy. Some view any public talk of moral values as insensitive to those who come from traditions that may be at variance with American values. This objection is wholly unfounded. When it comes to values, a host of national surveys have shown that parents from all backgrounds want their children to be honest, respectful, caring, trustworthy, law abiding, responsible, and fair minded.[18] In my own work with schools and parents, I have never encountered parents who do not share a broadly common vision regarding the virtues and moral standards that they expect of children. But this general consensus too often remains unseen or unacknowledged by those who formulate school policies on matters that revolve around moral issues.

As a consequence, public schools have lost the capacity to discuss moral matters with students in ways that could help them acquire virtue. By refraining from moral language, schools not only abdicate their responsibility to teach virtue, they accomplish precisely the opposite, inadvertently imparting to students the cynical message that virtue is not an important life asset.

Once, when I was a guest on a National Public Radio talk show, a parent of a fifth-grade student called to discuss an incident that was highly upsetting to her but all too familiar to me in my travels to schools.[19] That week, her son had been sent home with a note informing her that he had been caught taking money out of his fellow students' backpacks. The mother quickly got on the phone to the boy's teacher, telling the teacher that she was appalled and that she couldn't bear the thought of her son stealing from his friends. The parent asked what she could do about this. To her surprise, the teacher responded by asking the parent to say and do nothing.

"We were obliged to inform you of what happened," the teacher said, "but now we wish to handle this in our own way. To start with, we're not calling this incident 'stealing,' which would give your child a bad self-image. We've decided to call what your son did 'uncooperative behavior'— and we've pointed out to him in no uncertain terms that he won't ever be very popular with his friends if he keeps acting this way." In her phone call to the talk show, the parent said that she had doubts about the effectiveness of this kind of message. She also said that her son ignored her efforts to counsel him about the matter. She sensed that he had "blown the whole incident off" without learning anything from it at all.

In its "professional judgment," the school had translated a wrongful act (stealing) into a strictly instrumental concern (losing popularity). By consciously avoiding the use of terms like "right," "wrong," and "stealing" (the literal descriptor of the student's deed), the school ran away from the use of a moral language. As a result, the message the school offered the boy was entirely amoral: "You should avoid actions that will make you unpopular". This is hardly a charter for a life of virtue.

The school took this course of action, it claimed, in order to save the child from a reprimand that might give the child a negative self-image as a thief. Now it is true that the child may have felt embarrassed if forcefully told that he committed the moral offense of stealing. But stealing was actually what the child had done; and stealing in any civilized society (not just ours) is deemed wrong in a moral as well as legal sense. The child needs to hear this if he is ever to learn the difference between virtuous and a disreputable behavior. Very likely the child may feel unpleasant emotions such as shame and guilt in the course of such feedback. This, in fact, would be a *benefit* of the feedback rather than a detriment: such experiences in first-hand shame and guilt are precisely what researchers have found to be one of the most effective means of moral learning.[20]

The hesitancy to use a moral language is the most stubborn and distracting point of resistance for educating students for virtue in today's schools. The resistance is based on a number of misconceptions that persist despite their lack of support in evidence or in logic. Teachers worry that a moral reprimand could shame children, wounding their self-esteem. Some teachers believe that there are no standards of moral truth anyway; that it is hypocritical to preach moral standards to the young when so many adults ignore them; or that in a diverse society, one person's moral truth is another's moral falsehood. Yet it has been established beyond doubt, in both theory and research, that adult expressions of clear moral standards are precisely what guides the development of character and virtue in the young.[21]

Unfortunately, as I discuss in the following sections, even the character-education enterprise has been susceptible to our culture's contemporary aversion to moral language. This is an ironic turn of events that might seem amusing if the stakes were not so high. A review by Marvin Berkowitz and Melinda Bier has found that the most common topic in contemporary character-education programs is "social-emotional content," such as "personal improvement/ self-management and awareness," "relaxation techniques," and "emotional awareness."[22] Exactly which part of a child's moral development might be stimulated by training that heightens states of relaxation or emotional awareness is a mystery to me. Such states have little to do with the acquisition of morality. In fact, a pedagogy built around personal sentiments may well distract children from the real challenges of forging character.

So even in the midst of character education lies yet another hazard, born of the same errant ideas that fostered the problem in the first place. Some approaches to character education today have been misled by the trendy notion that children's positive feelings are the key to learning of all sorts, moral as well as academic. Sometimes this notion results in little more than silly activities meant to boost self-esteem; but when the effort to do that interferes with moral instruction, it goes beyond the silly to the harmful. This is unfortunate, because character education done in right way is a necessary part of the solution.

Schools can and should implement the kinds of character-education programs that teach students what virtue is, how it is used, and why it is important. This kind of instruction is an essential complement to the rules and expectations that schools should present to students through the kinds of practices I have discussed above. Good instruction about virtues does not happen automatically: it requires a conscious effort to put in place clear lessons that teach the moral dimensions of virtue. Useful methods for this exist, and some schools are succeeding in the mission of teaching students about virtue. But too many schools today are falling short, and some are teaching it in a wrong-headed way that does more harm than good.

Indeed, the overall agenda of American education has been moving away from the crucial mission of virtues and character education for well over a half century, and it is accelerating at the present time. Most troubling is that so few influential policy makers in the United States today consider moral and civic virtue to be priorities for the kinds of schools they are trying to promote.

In the following sections, I show how schooling in America is departing from its crucial (and traditional) mission of teaching students about moral and civic virtue. I begin by addressing a question that is asked so often, and in so many different ways, that if left unanswered, the question itself can become an intractable obstacle: should schools—especially public ones—be in the business of educating for virtue?

Should Schools Be in the Business of Educating for Virtue?

Although there is little argument about whether religious and home schools have a mandate to engage in moral education, some social critics have drawn the line there, insisting that values have no place in public school instruction. Critics of public schools' attempts at education for virtue (or character education) have come from across the ideological spectrum. Progressive educators have worried that such attempts amount to authoritarian indoctrination that could trample students' capacities to make autonomous moral judgments.[23] Traditionalists have complained that character-education programs in today's schools are promoting a fuzzy assortment of individualistic and self-centered values that not only will undermine the social fabric but could even lead to what one critic has deemed "the death of character."[24]

Other objections to character education have come from moral relativists who believe that there are no universally valid virtues worth promoting, from devotees of rational-self-interest theory who consider any moral ideas to be mere rationalization and thus a waste of time; and from strict members of faith communities who would like to keep the teaching of moral values within the province of church and family.[25] Accompanying all such objections is the unstated question, "Whose values do schools presume to teach, anyway?" Such a question reflects a deep skepticism about whether common moral values and a shared sense of the public good still exist in America.

Adding further to present-day reservations about character education in our public schools is a lack of agreement about what the proper focus of character education should be. Some (myself included) take the position that character education should focus on basic moral virtues of the sort that I identified in Chapter 1—moral virtues such as honesty, responsibility, respect, compassion, and fairness. But many in recent years have been using the umbrella of character education to cover a host of social-emotional "competencies" that have little or no moral significance. They include a range of social skills that can be used for either good or ill: for example, problem solving, self-awareness, social bonding, self-efficacy, and emotional literacy, any of which could readily promote antisocial goals unless they are guided by a clear moral compass. By including this jumble of nonmoral skills in character-education programs, educators not only have confused the primary agenda of character education, they have also have weakened the effectiveness of the programs, thus throwing into question the mandate of schools to invest in such efforts.

A recent study by the federal Institute of Education Sciences is instructive in this regard.[26] Purporting to test the impact of character-education programs on children's social behavior, the study found little evidence of a relationship between seven selected programs and outcomes such as altruism, pro-social behavior, and avoidance of problem behavior. Not surprisingly, when the results of the study were released, they were reported by the media as casting doubt on the feasibility of teaching virtue in school. But an examination of the contents of the seven programs that were selected for study reveals learning agendas that included "social skills training," "social and emotional learning," "social dynamics training," "social information processing," "social problem solving," "peer networks," "social bonding," "goal setting," "emotional literacy," "social competence," and "interpersonal problem solving."

Now any expert criminal could benefit from such skills as much as someone trying to accomplish good. To the extent that these seven programs have a concern with moral virtue, that concern is blurred among all the other program aims. The federal study thus provides a poor test of how real character education influences students; yet it will almost certainly be used to diminish whatever minimal support educational policy makers provide for teaching virtue in our schools.

In the United States today, the national political leadership clearly believes that public schools should limit their goals to teaching students elementary skills required for employment and national competitiveness. Once called the

"Three R's," such basic skills now are known as literacy and numeracy. The leadership's operating assumption seems to be that a single-minded focus on these elementary skills— especially numeracy—will prepare students for the "STEM" subjects that open up careers in science, technology, engineering, and mathematics.[27]

I concur on the importance of ensuring that all our students master basic skills in literacy and numeracy, for many reasons that include career opportunities and national competitiveness. But the narrow focus on these skills squeezes out other essential learning goals that our schools need to accomplish for the sake of their students as well as our society. The education of students for moral and civic virtue is primary among these now-neglected learning goals.

Reservations about the importance of character education have powerfully shaped our current educational policy in ways that have radically altered both the mission and the practices of schools today. In fact, it is hard to overstate the extent to which our country's current approach to schooling departs from the great American tradition established in the nineteenth century and early parts of the twentieth. The once-unquestioned judgment that virtue and character should be central to every school's mission has now become an alien notion to the policy makers and experts who direct educational policies in the United States.

During the nineteenth century, when public schooling took root in this country, few doubted that schools should aim to foster moral character in students. Everything in the American "common school," from its disciplinary practices to its texts, reflected the widely shared assumption that every school bore a responsibility to teach society's core values to its students.

For example, from 1836 to 1922, McGuffey's *Readers* were by far the number one school reading text in the United States. In their many editions, the readers sold over 120 million copies. They presented, without hesitation or qualification, the moral code that their original author, the Reverend William Holmes McGuffey, believed essential for children to learn; and most adults of the time must have recognized the code as similar to their own, for there were few if any arguments in the public sphere about its use in schools. As exemplified through the readers' stories and dilemmas, the McGuffey code can be simply stated: a child should be respectful, honest, diligent, compassionate, temperate in food and drink, fair minded, and clean speaking. If this sounds a bit like the code of virtues Ben Franklin espoused in the writings cited in Chapter 1, that is no coincidence: in the early decades of the Republic, there was not much doubt that citizens of good will shared common values.

In education, a consensus surrounding common values, and the responsibility of schools to teach them, endured for many years subsequent to the establishment of public schooling. As late as 1901, the National Education Association proclaimed that "the fundamental consideration in any system of schools . . . is the development of moral character."[28] This was not just a call to add a few discussions about ethics and morality. It was a conscious determination, by the country's dominant organization of professional educators, that moral character should be the *fundamental consideration* of schooling. In little over a century since that time, we have departed about as far from this conclusion as is possible to imagine—and with predictably unfortunate results.

The McGuffey *Readers* still sell about one hundred thousand copies a year, mainly in home schools and traditional communities, such as the Amish and similar groups. For the most part, the morally driven lessons of McGuffey have been replaced by a very different sort of school reading text. Some of the newer texts explore personal feelings of growing up; some convey the charms of pets; some delve into problems among friends or family; and some are terrifically entertaining, with irresistible titles such as *How to Eat a Fried Worm* and *Snot Stew*. Well written, cleverly illustrated, and amusing the books may be; but stocked with clear ethical guidance they are not.

The change in reading texts has been neither accidental nor compartmentalized. Since the latter part of the twentieth century, academic expertise has come to overshadow virtue as public schooling's single-minded priority. Increasingly over time, public schools have become places where children are sent for the sole reason of learning academic skills. The assumption (now explicitly stated) is that it should be up to students to figure out, through their own autonomous choices, how to employ the skills they learn. School time is seen as too precious to spend on "non-academic" matters; and in any case, teachers may not be trusted to convey the right values to children.

There have been notable exceptions to this view; but in recent years, they have not gained enough traction to rectify the matter. A character-education movement took root during the last decades of the twentieth century, no doubt in reaction to widespread and disturbing indicators of misconduct among students. Not only were schools seeing increases in old standbys such as cheating and vandalism, but many schools were also torn by actual violence, gang behavior, and self-destructive drug and alcohol abuse. Spurred by a public recognition that our schools needed to concern them-selves once again with student virtue, character education gained a foothold in public schooling nationwide. By the early 2000s, over 80 percent of the states in the union had imposed mandates on public schools to incorporate char-acter education in some way. Federal support for such pro-grams was authorized under the Clinton administration and tripled in size during the Bush administration.

But in many public schools, the programs were never more than marginal—perhaps an hour or so of ethics lessons and recitation of virtues during a school week. Disappointingly, the present administration, despite pouring vast amounts of federal funds into spending on education, has reduced or eliminated support for even these minimal attempts at character education, with the lone exception of a new anti-bullying initiative—a worthwhile effort, to be sure, but hardly a sufficient program of instruction in the moral and civic virtues that young people need to acquire mature char-acter. By and large, the current trend in federal education support has focused ever more single-mindedly on instruc-tion in basic academic skills, to the exclusion not only of other important intellectual attainments such as the arts and history but also of key elements of character such as motivation, purpose, aspiration, and virtue.

Thus, in our present-day public discourse—and even more importantly, in actual practice—the argument over whether public schools should devote their time and effort to educating students for virtue has been won by the naysay-ers. Discussions about the need to attend to the values and virtues of students have disappeared from our educational and political discourse; and although almost every school pays some lip service to its concern for students' ethical conduct, few sponsor serious programs in character education that go beyond an occasional class, part of a class, or special event.

Yet the need for character education will never go away. Despite the current complete lack of attention to it, all schools undeniably envelop their students in a moral climate of one sort or another, whether wholesome and uplifting or corrupting and dispiriting. The choices that a school makes (or *fails* to make) about its moral climate inevitably leave lasting marks on all students who attend the school. Character education, in the phrase of one seminal book on the matter, "comes with the territory."[29]

Imagine a school that really did try to stay out of the character-education business entirely, refraining from promoting virtues such as honesty or values such as a respect for authority, social rules, and orderliness. Apart from the chaos that would surely ensue in the school, would we not also expect the character of its students to be affected by the adverse message that such an exercise in moral abdication would impart? Students are always watching, and they soak up unspoken messages at least as avidly as they learn the explicit lessons they are taught.

In the end, the question is not whether a school chooses to provide its students with a moral education. All schools do so, whether they know it or not. But will a school do that *well*, consciously examining its practices with an eye to the messages they impart to students and offering programs that students can take seriously? Or will the school choose to look the other way, ignoring the negative affects of its practices on the growth of its students?

The Mandate for Virtue and Character Education

It is clear what is needed: public schools must accept their mandate to educate for character. Because they inevitably shape student character whether or not they consciously attempt to do so, schools need to take special efforts to do a good job at it. This requires presenting students with standards expressed in a moral language that sharply distinguishes right from wrong. In addition, schools must implement policies that directly demonstrate, and consistently enforce, these standards.

All of a school's implicit and explicit messages to its students—the hidden curriculum of practice as well as the stated curriculum of instruction—must direct student behavior towards these standards. Personal sentiments, such as wanting to be popular or "feeling good about myself," cannot stand as sufficient reasons for a moral choice. School officials and teachers must help students understand that they are expected to be honest, fair, respectful, and compassionate, whether or not doing so makes them feel good instantly in any particular situation. The virtues that schools should cultivate in students must transcend whatever personal feelings of the moment the students may have.

Work and Citizenship

American society has long benefited from the commitment of its citizens to work industriously at their chosen vocation and to dedicate themselves to service for the nation whenever such sacrifice is called for. The virtue of hard work has been called "the work ethic"; the virtue of dedication to the nation's needs, "patriotism." For most of American history, schools promoted these virtues without doubt or hesitation.[30] It was taken as a matter of course that hard work and patriotism were in the public interest, and that the public schools therefore had the responsibility to cultivate such virtues. This was accomplished in dozens of improvised ways throughout the school day: extra work when a teacher spotted a shoddy performance (including staying after school for repeated drills), exhortations, songs, ceremonies, awards, patriotic routines such as songs and skits, and multiple other intentionally symbolic gestures.[31]

It is difficult if not impossible to find any such methods employed in public schools today. Part of the problem is functional: the schools have been stripped of these "extras" due to union regulations, financial constraints, and the increasingly single-minded focus on testable basic skills. But an additional part of the problem is cultural: virtues such as the work ethic and patriotism are out of step with mainstream sensibilities in contemporary US education.

The results of this change are not hard to detect. Regarding the work ethic, surveys have found that barely more than a quarter of American students place top priority on working hard, compared with over three-quarters of Japanese youth.[32] Interest in citizenship and civic dedication ranks dead last among sources of purpose for American students.[33] In addition to such data (which, revealingly, are somewhat sparse, due to the profession's lack of attention to such matters), anecdotal accounts of desultory students abound. For example, a December 2009 column in *The Boston Globe*, bearing the title "My lazy American students," reported the following observation: "Teaching in college, especially one with a large international student population, has given me a stark—and unwelcome—illustration of how Americans' work ethic often pales in comparison with their peers from overseas."[34]

Such complaints are so common among teachers in American schools and colleges these days that PBS produced an award-winning documentary on the matter, entitled *Declining by Degrees*.[35] The film shows vast numbers of today's college students sleeping through classes, shirking their assignments, partying many nights of the week, and avoiding anything that bears a slight resemblance to schoolwork. Although meant as a sharp critique of current educational practice, the portrait it offers of American students' work habits is equally revealing.

Civic Virtue

Civic virtue requires a commitment to contribute to and if necessary sacrifice for the good of one's society—in the words of President John F. Kennedy, to "ask not what your country can do for you, but what you can do for your country". In recent years, not many public leaders have been urging young Americans to adopt this attitude or the civic virtue it implies. Indeed, the idea of devotion to one's country—the very concept of patriotism, which the great philosophers of ancient Greece believed to be essential for the social good—has been out of fashion in American cultural life since at least the Vietnam War. I will discuss this problem in depth in the following chapter. For now, I will simply note some of it signs in education today.

When teachers reflect on the idea of patriotism, they often confuse it with the kinds of chauvinistic and militaristic passions that were fomented by totalitarian ideologies such as National Socialism. Teachers have not abandoned patriotism as a value; most have a sense of it in their own lives. But it is rarely advocated as a legitimate goal of education or promoted as an essential virtue to pass on to students. When the subject does come up in education, it is usually to advocate ways to guard against its dangers. Many educators see patriotism as antithetical to a more global perspective on humanity and as the enemy of humane values such as peace and justice. As I will discuss in the following chapter, influential intellectuals have urged schools to teach children to become "citizens of the world" rather than to identify themselves with any particular nation-state. These views are widely shared by teachers in the ranks of our public schools, and they set the tone for much of what is taught in social studies curricula.

Why should this be troublesome? After all, the notion of global citizenship is a benign one, especially in a world that is growing closer together every day. Moreover, spirited criticism of our own country is healthy, absolutely in line with our democratic tradition. My concerns here are not with criticism per se but with its use in educating young people about civic understanding and virtue during the elementary and secondary school years:

- A positive emotional attachment to a community is a necessary condition for sustained engagement in it. For full, participatory citizenship in a democratic society, a student needs to develop a love for the particular society and its traditions, including its historical legacy and its founding principles.

- The capacity for constructive criticism is an important requirement for life in a democratic society; but if it is to develop into mature judgment and behavior, this capacity must build upon a prior, sympathetic understanding of that which is being criticized.

Students need a positive exposure to the history, cultural heritage, core values, and operating principles of their society if they are to become motivated to participate as citizens. To develop civic virtue, they need to acquire a love of their society, a sense of pride in its best traditions, an emotional affiliation with the broader community of state, a sense of patriotism in the most benevolent and inclusive senses of that word. What's more, students must be presented with a sympathetic understanding of the aims and workings of a democracy if they are to become its constructive critics.

All this should be done through action as well as words, in multiple contexts, and in ways that inspire emotionally as well as intellectually. As I discuss in the following chapter, we are very far from this goal with respect to the way we represent the American tradition to young people today.

CHAPTER THREE

Abandoning the American Tradition

Oikophobia—*the felt need to denigrate the customs, culture, and institutions that are identifiably "ours."* —*Roger Scruton*

The American tradition is grounded in ideals such as liberty and equal rights, as set forth in the Declaration of Independence, the Constitution, and other seminal founding documents. In addition, the tradition includes widely shared values that have evolved over the course of the American experience—for example, innovation, optimism, and a devotion to the broader common good that has been expressed by the motto *E Pluribus Unum.* Although never perfectly realized, such ideals and values have provided direction, purpose, and social coherence for citizens of the United States.

The inclusiveness of the American tradition has made it evocative to people from all backgrounds. Native-born and immigrant citizens alike have welcomed their identification as Americans, generally recognizing that this identification carries with it a moral stance deriving from the nation's legacy of freedom, equal rights, and devotion to the common good. To be sure, the American tradition does not mandate any particular political positions. But it does imply a commitment to the ideals that have shaped the nation's historical record. Our legacy of noble ideals is enduring, transparent, and fully available to all who wish to embrace it. People from throughout the world have chosen to do so, either by coming to America themselves or importing the ideals of liberty and equal rights into their own societies.

The American tradition, along with the stories of sacrifice and accomplishment by people who have brought the tradition to life over the course of the nation's history, has throughout the generations served as a source of inspiration and pride for young Americans. But in recent years, the tradition has not been communicated to the younger generations in any compelling or reliable manner. This has created a problem not only for the civic development of the young but also for the tradition itself, since it is the younger generation that one day must bear the responsibility for preserving and advancing it.

This chapter examines the way in which the American tradition is being represented—and too often denied or *mis*represented—by the adults and their institutions that shape the attitudes of the youth population. The primary institution that I examine is the American school. The central question that I ask is whether today's schools are conveying the American tradition to students in anything more than a shallow, biased, or perfunctory way.

American Identity Disparaged

A young person's orientation toward the American tradition directly influences one of the most crucial psychological choices that young people must make: how to identify themselves. It is well established in developmental science that the period when most of us acquire our personal identities is the formative years between adolescence and early adulthood.[1] Once established, a personal identity provides stability, motivation, and a sense of direction in life.

All kinds of choices flow from the kind of identity a young person acquires. Among the most important choices are civic ones. Some examples: whether being an active citizen is a defining part of who one is or wants to be; what being a citizen means for the manner in which one conducts one's social life; what (if any) civic causes to dedicate oneself to; and whether to participate constructively in the governing process, as opposed to simply complaining, stepping back, and letting others run the show.

A person's identity determines the types of interests he or she will pursue. People who advance their interests through civic and political means develop a sense of themselves as participatory citizens. Over time, a strong civic identity promotes commitment to participation in the governing process. There are three converging reasons why people who have strong civic identities choose to participate actively: to pursue their own interests and those of people with whom they identify; to fulfill a sense of "civic duty" or obligation to the common good; and to maintain their senses of themselves as responsible and effective citizens.[2]

Beyond civic identity in general, people usually acquire a more particular sense of self as a citizen of a nation. For people living in the United States, this means an identity as an American.[3]

A fiery debate about the meaning of American identity has occurred recently within the field of political theory—an indication of how charged, contentious, and consequential this notion has become. To do justice to the nuances of all the arguments would require a lengthy volume in itself. For the purposes of this short book, I simply refer here to one quote from this literature, an eminently sensible statement by the historian Philip Gleason that highlights the main points that I draw upon in discussing how today's young are wrestling with the question of American identity. Gleason comments that, for much of the history of the United States, "To be or to become an American, a person did not have to be of any particular national, linguistic, religious, or ethnic background. All he had to do was to commit himself to the political ideology centered on the abstract ideals of liberty, equality, and republicanism."[4] In other words, the ideals and values implicit in the American tradition, rather than facts of geography or cultural background, have shaped the substance of people's identification as Americans over the course of our history.

Significantly, social-psychological research has confirmed the present-day validity of Gleason's historical observation. One recent study showed that young people's conceptions of a "true American" are far more likely to revolve around ideas and values such as "to respect America's political institutions and laws" and "to treat people of all races and background equally" than around situational factors such as "having been born in America."[5] Another study found that, even among newly arrived immigrants, the ideas and values of the American tradition are the most salient features of their new identities as Americans.[6] "Being American is consistently associated with the themes of rights, freedom, and opportunity," the study reports.

Why is this important? Young people's ideas and values concerning their country prepare the ground for the civic components of their personal identities. A young person who understands the American tradition is more likely to develop a positive identity as a United States citizen than a young person who is ignorant of the tradition. Understanding and appreciation lead directly to a sense of commitment and civic action to support the society. When the young person decides that "the kind of person I am" is one who cares about his society, the result is a willingness to make the sacrifices required to preserve and enhance the society. That young person acquires a respect for the ideals and values the tradition embodies and feels a commitment to act in the manner required to promote them. This is the developmental source of civic virtue. For this reason, American identity is linked to the virtues that sustain our free society through the character development of young Americans.

During periods in American history characterized by a strong national purpose, positive civic identity came readily to young Americans. Members of the so-called Greatest Generation, which came of age during World War II, have been celebrated for their lifelong service to American civic society.[7] In their case, civic action sprang from a positive identification with the American tradition and a sense that it was under attack by totalitarianism and other common enemies.

A positive sense of American identity also can lead young people toward civic action in cases where the action reflects disapproval of current national policy. Research studies of college-age students who traveled to Mississippi for the civil rights movement during the "Freedom Summer" of

1964 has found these students to be exceptionally active in civic affairs later in life.[8] Far more than comparable members of their age group, they have continued to contribute extensively to social and political causes as they have grown older. Most of their later activity has been reformist in nature, critical of the national status quo. But in a broader sense, these students had a highly positive view of America and a strong sense of themselves as citizens who enjoyed the opportunity to work for social change. They were moved to action by their perception of a discrepancy between the nation's noble ideals and present-day realities. It was their faith in these ideals, their sense of obligation as Americans to fight for them, and their disappointment in the gap between the ideals and reality that spurred their civic commitment.

Despite its clear importance in motivating civic commitment among the young, the notion of positive American identity has come under sharp attack in many influential circles of our intellectual culture today. Many opinion leaders in education, business, and the mass media now embrace the assumption that the inevitability of globalization requires a worldview that ignores national boundaries. According to this view, we have come to a fork in the road between nationalism and global citizenship, and to achieve personal and societal success, the choice must be the global option. One recent statement of this now-prevalent point of view has been advanced by a law professor in a book about the future of citizenship. "Longstanding notions of democratic citizenship are becoming obsolete," the author argues, "even as we cling to them. . . . American identity is unsustainable in the face of globalization." As a replacement for a commitment to a particular nation-state, "loyalties . . . are moving to transnational communities defined in many different ways: by race, ethnicity, gender, religion, age, and sexual orientation."[9]

Consequently, in the name of a global future, many opinion leaders are presenting us with a choice between American and "transnational" or "global" identities. But that choice is both unnecessary and counterproductive. It can lead to disregard for the unique virtues and hopes that America has given the world. Moreover, it is an untenable choice for the essential educational mission of preparing young Americans for a life of civic commitment and purpose.

To educate young Americans for such a life requires a positive and inclusive vision of American identity. Of course, it is true that American identity has never been a simple matter. The creation and sustaining of the United States always required a delicate balance between regional affiliations and loyalty to the nation. That balance has not always been achieved, and it broke down in a bloody fashion during the Civil War. Tensions between regions, states, and national interest still persist and no doubt always will in some form or other. Moreover, beyond regionalism, the United States has always had an enormous amount of ethnic, religious, cultural, and ideological diversity, and this diversity is increasing to this day. At first glance, such diversity might appear to complicate the problem of American identity.

Yet despite these seeming divisions, the union has held, and few doubt its strength, even in our most fractious political times. Moreover, during times of national crisis, Americans usually pull together without hesitation. Anyone who walked the streets of Manhattan after the September 11 attacks could not help but be struck by the numerous displays of support, jammed into virtually every crack and alcove in the metropolis and rushed from every region of the country—including "heartland regions" often skeptical of New York City lifestyles.

Most importantly, a consensus has developed in the United States around the belief that diversity is our strength. It is now commonly recognized that diversity has been a positive force in American life. This uniquely positive American orientation toward diversity stems in large part from the principles reflected in the founding documents, which established a climate of liberty and opportunity for all, making possible the successful inclusion and advancement of émigrés from all parts of the world.

At one time, the term for such inclusion was "assimilation," a word that came to encompass the optimistic assumption that people from diverse backgrounds could assume a shared American identity. In recent years, the concept of assimilation—along with its more colorful metaphoric form, "the melting pot"—has gone out of fashion because of objections that such notions imply that all citizens must strip away every vestige of their original cultural identity if they wish to think of themselves as Americans. The objections have had some merit. When taken to an extreme, the notion of assimilation made unnecessary and unrealistic demands on new citizens' efforts to transform themselves into devoted Americans. It implied that an identification with one's ethnic heritage must conflict with American identity and therefore that the identity must be somehow suppressed or forgotten. For example, at the beginning of the twentieth century, a group of social reformers dedicated to incorporating Indians into mainstream American society celebrated a public statement made by an Indian youth at the time: "I believe in education because I believe it will kill the Indian in me and leave the man and the citizen."[10] Not only do such sentiments do violence to every individual's need to sustain deep personal affiliations, they disregard the many benefits that arise when a society expands its cultural horizons by respecting (and learning from) the best practices and traditions of its new members.

But we should treat the supposed opposition between ethnic and American identity as nothing more than a politically charged straw man. In actuality, immigrants to the United States normally have retained some ethnic identification, and they have expressed pride in their joint identities as "hyphenated" Americans. Indeed, social science research has found that immigrants who retain a sense of attachment to their native lands are the *most* likely to adopt positive identities as Americans, complete with strong patriotic sentiments and full participation in the civic society.[11] Contrary to conventional wisdom, these studies also have consistently shown that the children who maintain strong ties to their native communities are those most likely to become eager American citizens who participate actively in civic and community affairs.

This indicates that civic participation is a capacity that, once learned anywhere, is readily applied to American citizenship. The reciprocal of this conclusion is sobering: if we neglect to encourage this capacity in large segments of our own youth population, they may never become prepared to take on the responsibilities of citizenship.

In our time, inclusive notions of assimilation and the melting pot have been displaced in favor of separatist metaphors, such as "salad bowl," that explicilty advocate ethnic division.[12] As I noted above, the extreme versions of assimilation were not tenable; but this does not imply that we should move to the opposite extreme of separatism. In many corners of today's culture, however, the view that preserving ethnic identification means opposing American identity and rejecting any allegiance to the US national interest has won out. This radically separatist perspective presents a serious complication for the preservation of American identity as well as a severe threat to *E Pluribus Unum*. It also poses an intractable obstacle in the quest to educate young people for civic virtue, because it removes the motivational force provided by a positive American identity and the enduring commitment to ideals such as liberty that this identity implies.

Adding to these recent cultural points of resistance is a concern that celebrating American identity might unleash a chauvinistic desire to dominate the world. Images of militant nation-states pursuing mad paths of conquest are invoked to curb this allegedly menacing beast. But the United States makes for an unlikely example of a nation bent on world conquest. Although it can without doubt be argued that at times our country has thrown its weight around in a bellicose manner, American history is far more a narrative of restraint of power than of belligerence. The United States is known more for restoring its defeated enemies' fortunes than for remaining in place as colonizers; and its few attempts at colonizing were done reluctantly and after strident national debate.[13] As for the bellicose moments, as philosopher Jacob Needleman has written, "a nation that takes seriously its role in protecting its citizens cannot be obliged to act selflessly and meekly in the jungle of the world it lives in, like a community of saints or spiritual aspirants."[14] In this sense, the belligerent outbursts must be perceived in the context of a nation that generally has wielded its enormous power with restraint in a world full of very real enemies.

The Founders themselves were careful to avoid chauvinistic claims of superiority for the new nation, pointing out that the ideals that shaped it were universal, drawn from the world's great philosophers, and belonging to people anywhere who wished to follow their lead. Indeed, a suspicion of militant chauvinism has been a prominent theme in American thought from the outset. Ralph Waldo Emerson, who at times waxed reverential about his love for American ideals, set the skeptical tone regarding arrogant nationalism when he wrote, "The spread eagle must fold his foolish wings and be less of a peacock."[15] This spirit of skepticism and restraint has been as much a part of America's cultural heritage as has been a quest for global influence. As the British journalist Harold Evans has written of American national objectives throughout the twentieth century, "nationalism . . . was not merely tempered by self-interest. It was replaced by a vision of leading a plurality of like-minded nations, if necessary at a sacrifice."[16] Young people who learn about the history of the United States in an accurate manner will have little reason to see American identity as a badge of shame.

The Contested Virtue of Patriotism

Civic knowledge and understanding are important for informed citizenship. But there is an emotional side to citizenship as well. In recent times, unlike during most of American history, this has become contested and thus problematic. The problem centers on the notion of patriotism, now viewed as an obstacle to progress in many of our most elite intellectual, cultural, economic, and educational quarters.

The indicators of this are omnipresent, almost jarringly so. On the very day I sat down to write this section (July 5, 2010), *The New York Times* ran a "bloggingheads" piece entitled "Down with Patriotism?" In conventional journalistic practice, the *Times* assigned one pro and one con speaker to the task of debating the question. Somewhat predictably, the speaker who was opposed to patriotism declared that "this is not a form of allegiance that people need." (Mysteriously, this speaker also declared that "people got along fine" in the sixteenth and seventeenth centuries before the idea of patriotism was invented—a claim that might have raised some eyebrows during at least one thirty-year period in Europe). That speaker went on to assert that patriotism "motivates more death than justice" and, in our own case, would only propagate "the myth that America stands for the rule of law and stands for democracy."

I suppose this is fair enough—or at least to be expected—from a critical perspective. More surprising to me were the views of the speaker who was assigned to speak *in favor* of patriotism. The strongest endorsement he was willing to make in support of patriotism was that it may be excusable as an "irrational affection" and that it serves the valid purpose of getting the public to defer to whatever constitution their society happens to have adopted. This was hardly a full-throated call for love of the American tradition or appreciation for the noble ideals the tradition advances.

Although *The New York Times*'s bloggingheads debate is only one data point, in my informal observations of public discourse, it pretty much captures the spectrum of acceptable opinion about patriotism among mainstream intellectuals these days. This range of acceptable opinion goes from absolute hostility to anything smacking of national pride to defensive apologies for "understandable" affections for homeland and American lifestyle. It is hard to find among the intellectual class any unabashed celebration of American ideals, of American progress toward the realization of those ideals, or of any other landmarks of the American tradition.

In education today, the concept of patriotism has joined the ranks of the most politically incorrect terminology. Many educators at every level of schooling see patriotism as antithetical to a global perspective on humanity, and thus an enemy of the humane goals of peace and justice. Influential educators have urged schools to teach children how to become "citizens of the world," adopting a "cosmopolitan" perspective rather identifying themselves as Americans.

One prominent advocate of cosmopolitanism in education has been University of Chicago professor Martha Nussbaum, who has written that schools should avoid instilling in students an "irrational" patriotism "full of color and intensity and passion." In her book of essays questioning "love of country," Nussbaum wrote that "through cosmopolitan education, we learn more about ourselves." She went on to explain:

> One of the greatest barriers to rational deliberation in politics is the unexamined feeling that our own preferences and ways are neutral and natural. An education that takes national boundaries as morally salient too often reinforces this kind of irrationality, by lending to what is an accident of history a false air of moral weight and glory.[17]

Nussbaum therefore asked why we would ever teach American students to see themselves first and foremost as US citizens:

> Most important, should they [our students] be taught that they are, above all, citizens of the United States, or should they instead be taught that they are, above all, citizens of a world of human beings, and that, while they happen to be situated in the United States, they have to share this world with citizens of other countries.[18]

The posture that American citizens simply "happen to be situated in the United States" is about as far away from a sense of national affiliation as one can get. But Nussbaum is no more extreme in her distaste for US (or any other) attachment than many other prominent educators. Amy Gutmann, a brilliant, highly-respected political scientist, wrote in a reply to Nussbaum that students should be taught the "rights and responsibilities of democratic citizenship" rather than that they are "above all, citizens of the United States." Gutmann declared, "If most nations effectively taught human rights, practical reality would be immeasurably better than our present reality. The same cannot be said for basing education on shared national values, whatever those values happen to be. This nationalistic view is abhorrent."

Such a view, of course, dismisses the elevated and universal nature of the ideals embodied in the American tradition—a unique national tradition that actually has brought these ideals to life in the "practical reality" that Gutmann cares about. Instead, with less than complete understanding of how children really acquire a concern for civic virtue, Gutmann advocates that "all children—regardless of ethnicity, religion, gender, race, or class—should be educated to deliberate together as free and equal citizens in a democracy dedicated to furthering social justice for all individuals, not just members of their own society."[19]

Similarly, in his influential book *Banal Nationalism*, the British social scientist Michael Billig warned against any message, explicit or symbolic, that imparts a sense of national identity across generations: "Banal," Billig wrote, "does not imply benign. . . . In the case of the Western nation-states, banal nationalism can hardly be innocent: it is reproducing institutions which possess vast armaments."[20] Such sentiments have become shared by many teachers in the ranks of our schools. In fact, they set a tone for much of what is taught in social studies curricula in the United States today.

From a moral standpoint, there is certainly a case to be made that children should learn to examine and assess their own countries' policies in light of impartial standards of justice. This is how democracies avoid wrong turns, correct mistakes, and pursue progress in human rights and civil liberties. But Nussbaum's vision of a child forging an identity as a world citizen (whatever that is), or Gutmann's vision of children deliberating about justice "as free and equal citizens" blind to their own life conditions, conform to no known educational or developmental principles. They are no more than utopian fantasies. As such, they do little but distract us from the real and urgent task of cultivating civic purpose among the young.

Responding to the cosmopolitan perspective presented by Nussbaum, poet Robert Pinsky pointed out that such "sterile" notions of citizenship fail to "respect the nature of patriotism and similar forms of love."[21] Philosopher Michael

Walzer commented ". . . I am not a citizen of the world. . . . I am not even aware that there is a world such that one could be a citizen of it."[22]

What there is, of course, is a particular nation, called the United States, with a tradition of liberty, democracy, and a dedication to equal rights. Although imperfect in each of these regards—as are all human efforts—the tradition contains an abundance of achievements to admire and identify with. Many of them stem precisely from universalistic principles of justice that the critics of patriotism admire; but the actual achievements that advanced justice were made possible by passionate allegiances to real people and communities, and they were usually spurred by feelings of devotion to the American tradition.

As law professor Michael McConnell has written: "We do not suffer today from an excess of patriotism. . . . Few young Americans know much, or care much, about . . . even the aspirations of their own nation. Our problem is a lack of confidence in any vision of the good, and a lack of passion for anything beyond material gratification. . . . [C]osmopolitanism may turn out to be more destructive than constructive. It is more likely to undermine coherent moral education, which in the real world is rooted in particular moral communities with distinctive identities, by substituting a form of moral education that is too bloodless to capture the moral imagination."[23]

The Decline of Youth Civic Purpose

Debates among intellectuals bear more than academic interest in our society. They are reflected in consequential trends in education, which in turn are reflected in the minds and actions of our children. The lack of passion and commitment intrinsic to the cosmopolitan approach has contributed to a lack of civic purpose among large segments of today's younger generation. In a recent study, our research team found less than 1 percent of a sample of today's students expressing interest in pursuing careers of civic leadership.[24] Although some of these students considered themselves to be leaders among their friends, almost none of them desired to become a political candidate. One boy, for example, dismissed the prospect by saying, "It just doesn't seem like a very good job to me. I'd rather be concentrating on more artistic efforts rather than civic efforts or saving the world or something." For a democracy that relies on new cadres of talented youth to fills its leadership ranks, this is a grim tiding.

Talent is not a problem. The present generation of young people is as bright and talented as any in history, despite mythical labels such as "the dumbest generation." Their ability to create new technologies and other visionary inventions is impressive. Nor is the problem anything as oppositional as negative attitudes or rebellious worldviews. In my observations, most young people today are positively disposed toward their families, their communities, and their society. In an unformulated way, they are prepared to be patriotic—perhaps even more so than the generation that preceded them. They believe in service, and they want to make a difference in the world.

But there is a long distance between an unformulated sentiment and a life purpose. Civic purpose in a democratic society requires an understanding of how citizenship works and a sense of why it is necessary to get involved. Commitment to act on behalf of the common good requires a reason to care about one's society. In times of national need, such a commitment may demand serious personal sacrifice. Only patriotism, a love and appreciation for one's society, can motivate a willingness to sacrifice. This kind of devoted appreciation does not develop by itself. It must be cultivated through education and example.

To give living voices to the concerns I raise in this and the following chapter, I draw on interviews that my students and I have conducted with American youth over the past ten years, including interviews from the research that I referred to above.[25] These interviews focused on the aspirations of adolescents and young adults in our society, their beliefs about what is important in life, their attitudes toward our society, and their hopes and expectations for the future. The interview series culminated in January 2010 with questions about American identity and citizenship that were directed to a diverse sample of eighteen-year-olds.[26] Participants ranged from first-generation immigrant youth to children of families who have resided in this country for generations. As the interview responses show, a love of country and an appreciation of American identity are still alive among most American youth, but few have been prepared to do anything constructive about such sentiments. In a civic sense, the youth have been paralyzed both by the misinformation they have received and the essential information they have not received.

Beyond the lack of interest in civic leadership noted above, many of today's students view the notion of American citizenship with confusion and personal reticence. For example, in one of our studies, when one student was asked what American citizenship meant to him, he replied, "We just had that the other day in history. I forget what it was." Another

said, "I mean, being American is not really special. . . . I
don't find being an American citizen very important."[27] A
third replied, "I don't know, I figure it really shouldn't mean
anything." And a fourth said, "I don't want to belong to any
country. It just feels like you are obligated to this country. I
don't like the whole thing of citizen. . . . I don't like that whole
thing. It's like, citizen, no citizen; it doesn't make sense to
me. It's like to be a good citizen. . . . I don't know, I don't want
to be a citizen . . . it's stupid to me."

To the extent that political life shows up at all on many
students' radar screens, it is viewed with anxiety, suspicion,
or skepticism. "Most [politicians] . . . are kind of crooked,"
one of our student interviewees declared. Another, discussing national politics, said, "I feel like one person can't do
that much and . . . I get the impression that [most people]
don't think a group of people can do that much." The skepticism carried over to political action at all levels, including
school. When talking about how school government works,
one girl said, "The principal and vice principals probably
make the decisions and say what's going on and [tell you],
'Don't worry about it.'" Running through most students' attitudes about political participation is a palpable feeling of
futility, a "What's the use?" kind of sensibility,

Such statements, of course, are not universal. There
are young people today who dedicate themselves to their
local communities with strong feelings of obligation; and
there are those who serve in national organizations such
as AmeriCorps, the Peace Corps, Teach for America, or the
armed forces with pride in their contributions to society.
But such activities are far from the rule.

Virtually every study of US youth today has found large
pockets of apathy, skepticism, disengagement, and ignorance

regarding the American tradition. According to opinion surveys, only a tiny fraction of our youth population is now interested in leadership roles in local civic organizations.[28] In the survey results, it is hard to find a US public figure (other than in sports and entertainment) whom young people admire, let along wish to emulate.

In a US Department of Education study a few years ago, only 9 percent of American high school students were able to cite reasons why it is important for citizens to participate in a democracy, and a mere 6 percent could identify reasons why having a constitution benefits a country.[29] This decline in civic understanding has also been well documented in other surveys. For example, CIRCLE (The Center for Information and Research on Civic Learning and Engagement at the University of Maryland) reports that, from 1966 to 2002, interest in political affairs among college freshmen declined in a steady "step" fashion *by over half,* from 60 percent of the population to less than 30 percent.[30] These trends are unsustainable for a free society that relies on civic purpose, commitment, and virtue among its citizenry.

Just as it is important for young Americans to acquire the virtues that will enable them to live responsibly in a free society, so is it essential for them to develop an emotional allegiance to the nation that protects our freedoms. This allegiance is devotional in nature. Since the time of the ancient Greeks, and for much of our own history, it has been called, without hesitation or embarrassment, patriotism. Manifesting itself as a selfless love of country, patriotism is an indispensable motivator to action when a person is called upon to sacrifice for the national good. Patriotism has been responsible for the sacrifices that have won and saved American freedoms throughout history. As I noted in the Introduction, every struggle against our tyrannical opponents over the past two centuries, and all of our country's great moral campaigns, such the civil rights movement, were supported by strong patriotic sentiments and a love of the American tradition. A failure to convey such sentiments to young people leaves them unprepared for the active citizenship they will need to preserve liberty and democracy in the country they will inherit.

Historical Understanding, Student Interest, and the Anti-American Narrative

Teaching history can be difficult. Convincing students that they have something to gain by learning facts from faraway times and places is a major challenge. Even harder is conveying past events in ways that provide truthful accounts of what actually happened and how it has meaning for us in the present. It is impossible to do a perfect job at this; historical records are often ambiguous or obscure, and they may change as new documents emerge and new interpretations surface. But a good-faith, well-directed effort to teach the best available knowledge in a balanced manner can provide students with a sound foundation of historical understanding that will enable them to make informed civic judgments.

These days, some schools in the United States are rising to this challenge, taking seriously the concepts at the heart of our democracy and bringing to life the traditional American ideals of liberty and equal rights. Unfortunately, these programs are not the norm. They are more than matched by programs that are so misdirected or unengaging that they do more harm than good for a student's interest in historical truth.

Across the broad landscape of schools and colleges in the United States, the teaching of history is riddled with irregularity. An increasingly prominent part of the landscape is occupied by approaches that are driven by deliberate ideological agendas rather than by efforts to establish historical truth. Such approaches appear in many guises. Some emerge from the manner in which the subject matter of history is taught. Others spring from social studies, "global studies," "peace studies," and other mixed-discipline treatments of social problems such as international conflict, inequity, poverty, and environmental degradation. What many of these problem-centered approaches have in common is a shaky hold on the historical facts, a dismissive attitude toward objective truth, an explicit rejection of American national interests and foreign policy, and a relentlessly critical perspective on America's treatment of its own citizenry.

In discussing these approaches, I do not question their rights to be critical; nor do I question the motives of those who teach in this way. Indeed, critical thinking is among the finest parts of the American tradition. Speaking out when one perceives that one's country has taken a wrong turn is one of the finer signs of patriotism. My objection is educational in nature: this is no way to help students learn what they need to know in order to acquire the capacities and the motivation they need to become active citizens. It is the lack of pedagogical value in ideologically driven teaching that I address here, not the right to express dissenting opinions.

The background to the rise of ideologically driven history teaching can be found in a late twentieth-century educational movement to replace actual history courses with those involving social studies and similar curricula.[31] This movement was spurred by a belief that students need to acquire a global, rather than nationalistic, perspective, especially in the early years of schooling, when their attitudes about the world first develop. A social-science treatment of human behavior, it was reasoned, would advance a global perspective more than would a traditional historical one.[32] As a consequence, the teaching of history to students in the elementary and middle-school years was redirected toward the cosmopolitan education agenda that I discussed earlier in this chapter.

The explicit mission driving this shift was to "denationalize" conceptions of citizenship in favor of broader "basic human" notions of citizenship with global roots.[33] Educators who have promoted this shift often describe it as an attack on the entrenched interests of the world's power structures and a blow for "social justice."[34] Accordingly, there is little doubt that the shift has reflected an advocacy agenda driven by a particular ideology. The only real question is why such one-sided ideological advocacy has met so little resistance while shaping the teaching of such a consequential subject matter.

The purest example of this kind of ideologically driven teaching in history is the approach that has grown out of the late Howard Zinn's popular textbook, *A People's History of the United States*.[35] Although more extreme than the majority of social-justice-oriented teaching in place today, Zinn's approach has reached many students; and to at least a modest degree it is reflected in many of the less extreme but similarly oriented efforts. Together, these affiliated approaches have had a significant influence on history and social studies education in many parts of the United States.

The program that Zinn himself founded, called the "Zinn Education Project," has been backed by deep pockets of private support, and it has spread to school districts across the country: According to the project's website, the ZEP, has "partnered with 32 organizations to offer 31,000 teachers and teacher educators free packets for instilling the 'people's history' in schools. [It received] requests for its available 4,000 free packets, nearly half of which were sent to schools in California, New York, and Illinois."[36] In the ocean of American schooling, that amounts to a small inlet. But Zinn's book itself has had a far wider circulation. According to the publisher, *A People's History* has been "chronicling American history from the bottom up, throwing out the official version of history taught in schools. . . ." Although this may be something of an exaggeration (most public school history courses use other textbooks), Zinn's book and teaching materials can be found in numerous classrooms, from high school to university level, and other like-minded approaches are at least as prevalent.

The book is something of a phenomenon in its lopsided treatment of US history. It single-mindedly focuses on the sins of the American heritage, starting with Columbus and ending with Three Mile Island. And far from confining its critiques to generally acknowledged moral errors (slavery, discrimination, Indian removals, child labor) or even to policies and actions that have been considered debatable (Vietnam, Mexico, tax breaks for wealthy businesses and farms), the book takes America to task for actions that have been commonly accepted as sources of national pride. It questions American conduct during World War II, suggesting that US entry into the war was deceptive and ill motivated, the design of "a government whose main interest was not in stopping fascism but in advancing the imperial interests of the United States."[37] The book levels similar critiques at government policies during the Civil War, the Great Depression, the Cold War, and virtually every other conflict or challenge encountered since the arrival of Europeans on these shores. Indeed, it is hard to find within the pages of this book any redemptive actions by any people in positions of power during the entire panorama of US history.

To accomplish this epic feat of negativism, Zinn keeps the narrative free of against-the-grain events such as Washington's Farewell Address, Lincoln's Gettysburg Address, most achievements of science, the arts, faith and charitable organizations, industry, medicine, education, the labor movement, the civil rights movement, the Progressive era, and virtually all other American episodes that could yield a claim to promoting moral progress in this country. The book weaves a dark tapestry unbroken by points of light.

I do not question the intentions of Zinn or his educational project. Indeed, many years ago, I had a lengthy and fascinating conversation with Zinn about teaching history. He was open and generous with the time he gave to me as a beginning scholar. I found him to be man of sincere beliefs, an admirable willingness to stand up for his convictions, and an ability to advocate compellingly for his views. Yet I was convinced that he held a mistaken view of how young people learn and what they need to know in order to make sound judgments as citizens. In addition, I had reservations regarding his stance on the nature of truth: he expressed a post-modernist skepticism about the possibility of knowing anything objectively, asserting claims such as "there is no such thing as facts." Cordial though he was, he showed little interest in my contrasting perspectives on what students need to learn, and little sense of the importance of cultivating in students a respect for the search for truth in the face of the inevitable ambiguities and uncertainties that accompany human affairs.

My main objection to this view, then and now, is that a critical perspective is a poor starting point for any program of learning. Yes, critical thinking is an essential skill. But *prior* to criticism, students need to acquire a solid understanding of a subject and a reason to care enough about it to assume the hard task of mastering it. Criticism, when introduced, must be placed in a meaningful context; and this can exist only after students have fully understood that which is being criticized. In order to build a sound foundation for critical thinking, teachers must convey the positive case, emphasizing why the subject is worth criticizing in the first place. Only then will students be able to use critical thinking in an informed, intelligent, and constructive way.

By subjecting students to a starkly negative account of American history, Zinn's approach violates the very first principle of human development: anything that develops must grow out of something (or *"something is not growing out of nothing,"* to quote one famous developmental theorist).[38] Students must develop a positive understanding and sound appreciation of the history of American democracy if they are to acquire the ability to think clearly as citizens and exercise their judgments well. This is also essential in an emotional sense. Young people need to care about their society if they are to dedicate their concerted efforts toward citizenship.

In his writings, Zinn acknowledged hearing such objections from students. He wrote, "A high school student recently confronted me: 'I read your book. . . . [Now] how can I keep from being thoroughly alienated and depressed?'" This, Zinn admitted, is a good question, one that he heard often—along with another, equally important question and comment: "Don't we need our national idols? You are taking down all our national heroes." Here is Zinn's revealing answer: "Granted, it is good to have historical figures we can admire and emulate. But why hold up as models the fifty-five rich white men who drafted the Constitution as a way of establishing a government that would protect the interests of their class—slaveholders, merchants, bondholders, land speculators?"[39]

To describe the Founders in this manner is about as far from an inspiring—or balanced—introduction to American history as can be imagined. It fails to accomplish either of education's two key goals: providing students with an impartial body of truthful knowledge; and motivating students to use this knowledge responsibly for the benefit of themselves and their society. Why should a student bother to study the lives and achievements of long-dead men and women who pursued little more than petty, selfish interests?

As a history textbook, *The People's History of the United States* does have a noteworthy strength: it is lively and interesting to read. Unfortunately, this puts it in a miniscule number of the history texts currently in use in our schools. Chester Finn has described the textbooks that are most widely used as "fat, dull, boring books that mention everything, but explain practically nothing. . . . Because textbook publishers bend over backward not to offend anybody or upset special-interest groups," Finn says, "so much in today's history texts is simplified and sanitized."[40] Such lifeless treatments of history fail to capture the imaginations of American students, because they shy away from telling the stories of the actual dramatic conflicts and choices that shaped the American tradition.

Not surprisingly, most students in our country show virtually no interest in its history, and their lack of interest shows up in the spotty state of their knowledge. A recent survey by Common Core found that large portions of the seventeen-year-old student population have mistaken ideas about such fundamental historical matters as the Bill of Rights, the Civil War, *The Federalist* Papers, and the McCarthy/US Senate hearings.[41] A significant minority do not know who fought against the US in World War II and cannot identify Adolf Hitler. A prefatory note to the report from Common Core's executive director puts it in this rather astonishing way: "Senator Joseph McCarthy investigated people who protested the war in Vietnam, better known as the Second World War. Fortunately, that war was over before Christopher Columbus sailed to America; otherwise we might never have experienced the Renaissance. A new survey of 17-year olds reveals that, to many, the paragraph above sounds only slightly strange."[42]

The problem of low student motivation to learn history and civics is compounded by the distorted priorities of today's schools. Teaching about the national heritage of the United States has taken a back seat to just about every other agenda item in American education today. When the subject does comes up—often in the guise of a social studies curriculum oriented to "global understanding," "multiculturalism," and "peace studies"—the achievements and values of the United States over the centuries are downplayed in favor of the kinds of critical treatments I have noted above.

All too often, the subject does *not* come up, because so many schools have turned their exclusive attention to rudimentary skills of math and reading that show up on the politically prized national tests. Almost all educators know the limits of these basic skills and the insufficiency of these tests to gauge student's understanding of the most important issues in the lives they will pursue. But most schools have succumbed to political pressures from the federal government and have turned themselves into test-prep centers that leave students both uneducated and uninspired. As Antonia Cortese and Diane Ravitch have written, "the nation's education system, we believe, has become obsessed with testing and basic skills because of the requirements of federal law, and that is not healthy. . . . We have no doubt that the current mania for testing and test-preparation has narrowed the curriculum and caused the exclusion of such subjects as history, literature, civics, geography, science, and the arts."[43]

The result is a generation of young people in America who have been called "historically illiterate" by the US Department of Education's National Center for Education.[44] One recent indication of this, as described in a Scripps-Howard news report, was provided by the American Council of Trustees and Alumni, which commissioned the Roper Center to survey college seniors at the nation's top universities. "Four out of five, or 81 percent, of seniors from the top schools received a grade of D or F on an exam drawn from basic high school curriculum questions."[45]

Not only has the single-minded focus on basic and remedial skills driven the teaching of history and civics far down the ladder of our school priorities, it has also added to the present-day tendency, noted above, of teaching these subjects in a dull and lifeless way. Many schools present civics as merely an abstract set of principles that students neither understand nor care about.

Recently, a colleague of mine who is familiar with the State of California school curricula showed me the standards currently used to guide instruction and test students in eighth-grade civics. Here are some examples:

8.1.4. Describe the nation's blend of civic republicanism, classical liberal principles, and English parliamentary traditions.

8.2.4. Describe the political philosophy underpinning the Constitution as specified in the *Federalist Papers* (authored by James Madison, Alexander Hamilton, and John Jay) and the role of such leaders as Madison, George Washington, Roger Sherman, Gouverneur Morris, and James Wilson in the writing and ratification of the Constitution.

8.2.7. Describe the principles of federalism, dual sovereignty, separation of powers, checks and balances, the nature and purpose of majority rule, and the ways in which the American idea of constitutionalism preserves individual rights.

8.3.1. Analyze the principles and concepts codified in state constitutions between 1777 and 1781 that created the context out of which American political institutions and ideas developed.

We looked at each other in amazement, asking: *Is this really meant for eighth graders, not political science doctoral students?* In all the standards' nuanced treatments of political process, it was hard to see what any typical thirteen-year-old could possibly connect with. Missing entirely were insights about the kinds of issues that students experience in their own lives: governing play and games through social rules; establishing ways to arrive at fair solutions when peers disagree; respecting authority (including knowing how to determine whether a particular authority figure is legitimate); and the rights of those not in authority to obtain redress from legitimate grievances. Only when civics is taught through the lens of a student's own concerns and experiences can it come to life. When instruction is driven by standards so remote and complex that students will inevitably tune out, civics education becomes nothing more than a charade, another causality of the test-prep factory mindset.

Training Student Teachers in Anti-Americanism

In May 2005, according to a local New York City newspaper, students in the Brooklyn College School of Education complained that they were being pressured to adopt anti-American ideological beliefs they disagreed with.[46] In one class, according to a student's complaint, the instructor insisted that English must be considered the language of oppressors, because of the unjust imperialistic actions of the United States. According to this story, the complaining student said that he believed the course material to be illegitimate, and he also objected that students were forbidden to express their opinions on the matter. Adding to the pressure on the student, another instructor at the college stated that this student's complaint amounted to "aggressive and bullying behavior toward his professor" that should be considered a breech of the institution's standards of conduct for students in its teacher training program. After a stormy period of accusations and investigations, the incident was resolved by cooler discussions among faculty who were mindful of the college's tradition of academic freedom.

Although such out-and-out clashes over indoctrination claims have been relatively rare in the annals of American teacher education, they do indicate an ideological atmosphere that permeates many present-day teacher education programs. In fact, the source of the Brooklyn College incident apparently was a set of standards put in place by the powerful National Council for Accreditation of Teacher Education. In 2000, NCATE announced that it would henceforth base its accreditation of teacher education programs on standards that focus on "knowledge, skills, and dispositions" of teaching candidates. The focus on "knowledge and skills" was nothing new; it is the normal fare of educational assessment at all grade and professional levels. But the idea of assessing a candidate's "dispositions" opened the way to a new sea of ambiguity. NCATE's original definition, at use at the time of the Brooklyn incident, was as follows:

> **Dispositions.** The values, commitments, and professional ethics that influence behaviors toward students, families, colleagues, and communities and affect student learning, motivation, and development as well as the educator's own professional growth. Dispositions are guided by beliefs and attitudes related to values such as caring, fairness, honesty, responsibility, and social justice. For example, they might include a belief that all students can learn, a vision of high and challenging standards, or a commitment to a safe and supportive learning environment.[47]

It is certainly reasonable to expect teaching candidates to believe that all children can learn, and to be committed to high standards and safe environments. But it seems clear that NCATE also intended the term dispositions to signify beliefs and attitudes that reflect stances toward matters such as social justice that imply—or at least can be interpreted to imply—a specific ideological orientation. The construction "Dispositions are guided by beliefs and attitudes. . ." also implied that the candidate not only must *have* such beliefs and attitudes but must be *guided* by them as well. Thus the definition uses the word "disposition" for dual purposes, to indicate particular kinds of ideological beliefs and attitudes, and to indicate a tendency to be guided by them. This double meaning gives the definition a long reach as well as almost infinite ambiguity. In the Brooklyn College case, according to the news story, the instructor was reported to have linked the disposition standard to beliefs about social justice that included the highly disputable claim that the United States had been such a malicious force in the world that English must be deemed the language of oppressors.

Fortunately, as in countless other moments in American history, free speech saved the day. Members of the Brooklyn College faculty stepped forward to protest the hazardous looseness of the NCATE disposition standard, with one of them telling the newspaper: "All these buzz words don't mean anything until you look and see how they're being implemented. . . . Dispositions is an empty vessel that could be filled with any agenda you want." NCATE itself, possibly in response to this controversy, has revised its standard to omit direct reference to social justice. The organization's new standards are an improvement, although they do leave some lingering openings for instructors to insert their own interpretation of "beliefs and attitudes."[48] Vigilance on this point will still be required. But as Thomas Jefferson long ago reminded us, this is nothing new regarding matters of liberty in human affairs.

Beyond the eternal need to guard against infringements on free opinion rights, the Brooklyn College case reveals the dangers of anti-American bias in contemporary education. Some teachers believe that they are striking a blow for justice by describing the United States as a persistently immoral force in the world, that they are cultivating critical thinking skills in students and teaching them to question authority (although they sometimes do not seem pleased to have their own authority questioned, as in the case just discussed). Although critical thinking and the questioning of authority have well-honored places in any democracy, a constant stream of negative opinions will not persuade students to learn about their country or participate in its civic affairs. Nor will it convey anything like an objective and balanced view of US history.

Anti-American bias in teaching can accomplish only one thing: a failure to pass along the American tradition to new generations of youth. The sad irony, of course, is that our tradition of liberty and equality is being rejected in the name of human rights and justice. It is hard to imagine how this could advance the cause of democratic progress in the world.

It is certainly true that the world's people are becoming increasingly interdependent and that young people must learn to operate well on a global stage if they are to maximize their potentials for success. In a moral sense, too, it is essential that nations learn to work together harmoniously in an internationally-aware manner. Although globalization is not as new as many seem to think (recall Marco Polo), it is certainly here to stay. But none of this implies that citizens must reject, deny, or forget the finer elements of their national traditions. The American tradition has contributed vast benefits to the country's own citizens and to the broader world beyond. *Teaching* that tradition in a compelling and truthful manner is important for cultivating in young Americans the capacity to make sound judgments. *Honoring* that tradition is essential for fostering civic purpose and commitment to the common good among those same Americans. Far from removing them from the global stage, an education in the strengths and achievements of the American tradition will provide them with a foundation for interacting with the world in a morally grounded, optimistic, and purposeful manner.

CHAPTER FOUR

The American Dream Denied

The history teacher told us the American Dream was dead.
—Stephanie, high school senior, January 2010

A belief that America is a special place—or, to put it more precisely, that it stands for a special approach to social governance (the so-called "American Way")—has long been part of our national image. Some have questioned whether this image has any basis in reality. In the intellectual world, scholars have argued vigorously about whether the United States is indeed unique in the world. In academic discourse, this has been known as the debate over the claim to "American exceptionalism." Scholars on the skeptical side of this debate have pointed to the kinds of historical failings that, as noted in the previous chapter, some popular history textbooks have dwelled on. Scholars who argue in favor of American exceptionalism have countered by citing the success the United States had had in turning such cherished ideals as liberty and equality into political reality at home, and to the special role the nation has played in promoting the spread of political freedom around the world.[1]

Recently, this debate has become more than academic. A November 2010 front-page story in the *Washington Post* noted that: "'American exceptionalism' is a phrase that, until recently, was rarely heard outside the confines of think tanks, opinion journals and university history departments. But . . . the idea that the United States is inherently superior to the world's other nations has become the battle cry from a new front in the ongoing culture wars."[2]

Scholarly and cultural debates aside, the belief that there is something special about the American Way has endured in the minds of those, whether native born or immigrant, who live in the United States. Moreover, this belief shapes Americans' sense of their own special identity in the world. As historian Louis Masur has written, "Exceptionalism is above all else the story we choose to tell about ourselves . . . and in telling it, over and over, at times we even make it so."[3]

Liberty and equal rights, as noted above, are high on the list of the prized ideals that define the American Way. At home and around the world, America has been known for these and other closely associated qualities, such as individualism, opportunity, and innovation. Since the time of the American Revolution, it has been frequently said that the meaning of America throughout the world has been determined more by this set of ideals than by its geographical location. In this way, the United States indeed has been unique among nations.

Prominent among the defining elements of our national identity, and related to the ideals of the American tradition, has been the notion of "the American Dream." Again, this is a unique concept among nations: there is no "French Dream" or "New Zealand Dream." The term has become almost a mantra in American popular speech. Politicians, educators, the mass media, and social historians refer to it daily. But the meaning of the phrase has changed increasingly in recent times.

In current usage among opinion leaders, the American Dream has come to signify little more than the expectation of increasing material prosperity and the accumulation of sudden wealth. Moreover, in contemporary intellectual discourse, it is treated as either a vanishing ideal or an outright myth, and is rarely written about without a touch of irony, longing, or skepticism.

For example, Harvard sociologist Christopher Jencks writes that the American Dream revolves around the materialistic expectation that "this country is a place where anyone who builds a better mousetrap can get rich . . . [and] everyone who works hard and behaves responsibly can achieve a decent standard of living."[4] This is a well-phrased comment about one central component of the American Dream, but it ignores the more idealistic components of the Dream, such as the hope of leading a fulfilling life by freely following the dictates on one's own conscience.[5] Others who write about the concept go even further than Jencks in linking it to specific consumer attainments, such as home ownership and the two-car garage.[6]

Very often, social critics who ground their views in a one-dimensional, materialistic interpretation of the American Dream dismiss its authenticity. A popular book in recent years bore the emblematic subtitle "The Futile Pursuit of the American Dream". This characterization is largely in keeping with the consensus of scholarly thought on the matter.[7] One leading educator, writing about the prospects of urban youth today, writes that ". . . the American dream has died."[8] Like other contemporary commentators, he was referring to the Dream solely as an expression of materialistic aspiration.

Although it is true that the American Dream has always included a component of material aspiration, its material goals traditionally have been set in the broader context of an individual's search for personal and spiritual fulfillment. Historian James Truslow Adams crafted the original formulation of the concept in the early part of the twentieth century, and it still rings true, however distant it may seem from today's more materialistic versions. Adams phrased it as "that dream of a land in which life should be better and richer and fuller for everyone, with opportunity for each according to ability or achievement. . . . It is not a dream of motor cars and high wages merely, but a dream of social order in which each man and each woman shall be able to attain to the fullest stature of which they are innately capable, and be recognized by others for what they are, regardless of the fortuitous circumstances of birth or position."[9]

When Martin Luther King Jr. inspired the nation with his soaring "I Have a Dream" speech, he began by noting that "*it is a dream deeply rooted in the* American *Dream.*" Dr. King's dream, first and foremost, was a call for justice at a time when an important segment of the American population had been excluded from many of the freedoms enjoyed by their fellow citizens. He realized that this exclusion contradicted the American Dream. By referencing the latter in this seminal statement, he was invoking one of the defining principles of the American tradition, the promise of equal opportunity. Dr. King's allusion to this hallowed principle added power and depth to his landmark speech. The Dream offers every US citizen the chance to strive toward the aspirations they hold most dear, whether material, personal, social, or spiritual.

The idea that in the United States it is possible to start with nothing and achieve success—whether material, social, or personal—stems from an optimistic line of thinking reflected in the Horatio Alger stories of the nineteenth century. With grittily resolute titles such as *Struggling Upwards*, *Sink or Swim*, and *Luck and Pluck*, the stories portrayed a life in America that offered opportunity to all those who would seize it. Legions of young people read these stories during the decades after they were written, taking to heart the message that America is a land of promise for people who strive with good faith and persistence.

Yet in our time, the Horatio Alger approach to the American Dream has run into ridicule and dispute. It is now fashionable among scholars to refer to "the Horatio Alger Myth," indicating their conclusion that social mobility in the United States is now more fiction than fact.[10] Several social critics have argued that, for major segments of the US population, the pursuit of the American Dream is pointless, because the economic power elite has rigged the system.[11] Among academic researchers, deep skepticism about the possibility of individual progress has become predominant: Horatio Alger and the American Dream are considered to be equally long expired.[12]

Teachers and students have been swayed by such ideas. For example, a high school student we interviewed for one of our recent Stanford studies stated that the American Dream "is just something people believed back in the older days. I don't know if it was ever right, but it doesn't make a whole lot of sense for me or my friends that I know." Another, quoted at the beginning of this chapter, told us that her class had learned from her history teacher that the American Dream had died, because prospects for success in this country have shriveled for all but the wealthy.

Whether or not economic and social mobility in the United States still exists for the majority of the population—and I will not express an opinion about that, since I am neither an economist nor a sociologist—it is a destructive and unnecessary mistake to convey a totally pessimistic message to young Americans: destructive because it discourages them from aiming for success at precisely the period in their lives when they are formulating their ambitions; and unnecessary because, whatever the current normative economic and social trends may be, such trends do not determine the fate of any particular individual. That is to say, whether or not normative data show economic mobility for many in the general population, it is certain that there will always be *some* people who find ways to gain success. And we know from a developmental perspective that if someone believes success to be unachievable, that person will *not* be among those who do manage to succeed.

For any individual, a belief that opportunity does not exist becomes a self-fulfilling prophecy. This is especially true for young people who are just forming their attitudes about the world and their prospects in it. It has been well established in recent psychological science that an optimistic attitude regarding future prospects is essential if a young person is to thrive in life.[13]

The discouraging message that "the American Dream is dead" because of alleged economic immobility in our society today is misleading in a more profound way as well. As

I noted above, the full meaning of the Dream encompasses aspirations that go far beyond material gain. Without question, that has been the case earlier in our history; and even in our money-oriented, media-addled time, vestiges of a more elevated vision of the American Dream endure among large segments of the population.

Certainly our forbearers would have thought it strange to confine their hopes for successful lives in America to the attainment of materialistic prosperity. Although early settlers in America always strived to provide well for their families, they did not equate happiness with accumulating the equivalents of glittering homes and automobiles. Until quite recently in our history, the American Dream incorporated expectations that went beyond, and were far more elevated than, the acquisition of personal wealth and status.

This was certainly true in the centuries prior to the coining of the phrase American Dream. In the faith-driven pilgrimage of the Puritan settlers, America was cherished as a place where one could feel closer to God than in the stultifying traditions of England and Europe. The real American Dream for those early settlers was to find happiness through spiritual salvation; it had little to do with attaining material wealth. As historian Andrew Delbanco has written, "Compared to the English Babylon the Puritans had left behind, New England was a wilderness barren of worldly comforts; but it was suffused by God."[14] In this physically harsh but spiritually rich environment, John Winthrop saw fit to write to his wife, "I never fared better in my life, never slept better, never had more content of mind."[15]

Waves of immigrants, all with their own, varied beliefs, joined the Puritan settlers in shaping the future of this new country. But the spirit of the sacred in American identity endured. Indeed, until well into the twentieth century, it was common for Americans to speak in reverential tones about their devotion to the nation—a devotion that Tocqueville noted "expands indefinitely when they think of the state."[16]

For young Americans, this devotion was vividly expressed during times of war. The letters and diaries of American soldiers from the Civil War through World War II show a widely shared, deeply felt conviction that sacrificing for the cause of American freedom should be considered a noble duty.[17] Moreover, devotion to "the land of the free" was regarded as not merely a duty but also a source of real happiness. Some of the passionate artwork from World War I expressed the romantic idea that the ultimate sacrifice—death in battle—could itself be a source of final pride and joy.[18] Iconic American writers such as Emerson and Whitman also wrote of the joys they found in their constant affection for the United States and its elevated ideals; and they alluded to the spiritual satisfaction they found in dedicating themselves to the "sacred nation" that pursued a transcendent set of aspirations in war as well as in peace.

At this writing, at the end of the first decade of the twenty-first century, the nation is fighting two international wars. There is very little consciousness of either war among the general youth population. Of course, there is one notable exception: the young men and women in uniform who have been sent to the battlefronts. The sentiments that these young people in uniform express are serious, dedicated, and loyal to their military units and fellow soldiers. Yet even among members of this group, we do not often see a conviction that they are dedicating themselves to the noble causes of freedom or democracy, or even that patriotic devotion to the United States has much to do with the sacrifices they are making.

The aspirations of these young men and women tend to center instead on career goals (the armed services as routes to good jobs), personal rewards (gaining skills, traveling around the world), and pride in wearing the uniform of an admired military unit.[19] If these young soldiers also view their services to the nation, and their potential sacrifices, as sources of pride and happiness, they do not usually mention it. For example, one young soldier interviewed in one of our studies spoke about his military service in this way: "It's got prestige that comes with it, and you can just say that you've got a real good job. . . . [T]he military offers me a chance to see the world. I've always wanted to go overseas, and I've never been able to." As they mature, this young man and his compatriots may discover a more fulfilling reason to serve; but at this point they show few indications that they connect their service with any broader national goals.

The degeneration of the American Dream from the spiritual to the material—and from the joy of devotion to the common good to the quest for personal gratification—is a giant step away from the kind of dedicated citizenry needed to preserve a free society. The problem of community disintegration in the United States has been written about from a number of angles: loss of social capital, isolation, alienation, and so on.[20] But the problem I refer to here goes more deeply into the individual consciousness, and it has a discouraging effect on the formation of character, especially among the young. These adverse psychological and character effects pose grave threats, not just to community solidarity in the United States but also to the political liberty that has defined the essence of this nation from the time of its founding.

Tocqueville anticipated precisely the threats to liberty posed by the self-centered and materialistic version of the American Dream that has predominated in our time:

> I seek to trace the novel features under which despotism may appear in the world. The first thing that strikes the observation is an innumerable multitude of men, all equal and alike, incessantly endeavoring to procure the petty and paltry pleasures with which they glut their lives. Each of them, living apart, is a stranger to the fate of all the rest; his children and his private friends constitute to him the whole of mankind. As for the rest of his fellow citizens, he is close to them but does not see them; he touches them but he does not feel them; he exists only in himself and for himself alone; and even if his kindred still remain to him, he may be said at any rate to have lost his country.[21]

To nourish and sustain civic virtue, people require hope: the expectations that striving, commitment, and sacrifice eventually will advance their good purposes, and that in some way or other, their virtuous choices will make a positive difference in the world. The American Dream, in its fullest and most profound sense, has generated among previous generations of the young extraordinary degrees of such hopefulness. The present-day derogation of the Dream, by limiting it to its most baldly materialistic components and then disputing the possibility of material progress, is a sure formula for the destruction of hope.

Hand in hand with the loss of hope comes a decline of trust in the American social compact. This decline has been documented in virtually every examination of Americans' changing attitudes towards their society and those who govern it. According to Pew Research Center data, during the 1950s almost 80 percent of Americans expressed trust in civic officials. There has been a steady decline since then, with a mere 22 percent expressing similar trust today. The current sense of mistrust, according to the Pew findings, goes way beyond skepticism regarding the poor performance of incumbent politicians. It has become a decline of hope and trust in the American Way and the American Dream, a loss that grows greater with each successive generation. If we teach young people that the Dream is dead, and that in any case it stood for nothing more than selfish and greedy consumerism, we are promoting that loss by teaching every generation that their efforts on behalf of their country are futile.

The danger that we could lose our country—this was the prescient warning from Tocqueville, the nineteenth-century observer who was right about so much else regarding American democracy. The warning is as fresh today as when he penned it. For us, Tocqueville's message bears meanings at least as serious as those he imagined. If we fail to transmit to the younger generation the devotion to country required for sustaining America's special ideals, we will lose our country by allowing its future to drift away through the indifference of its future stewards. Moreover, if we allow the ideals and aspirations embodied in the American Way and the American Dream to become degraded by cynicism, neglect, or ignorance of their meaning, we will lose our country's time-honored capacity to serve as a beacon of hope and liberty for ourselves, our future generations, and the entire world.

The New American Century

The early European settlers came to New England in search of freedom to pursue their own ways of seeking God. As

American life evolved over the centuries, that aspiration became part of an expanding catalogue of personal and political freedoms. Some of these were ingrained in the Constitution: freedom of speech; freedom to assemble, pursue economic aims, and move across social and geographical divides. Other key political liberties were added through later legislative and judicial rulings.

Over all this time, important parts of the population—women, African Americans, Native Americans, and many others—who had been excluded from political liberty gained new access to it. In each case, the boundaries of the American Dream were expanded to encompass legions of new constituents. Logically, this was simply a direct extension of the ideals in which the American Dream was rooted: individual liberty and opportunity for all. From early in the history of the United States, farsighted leaders saw it as an unsustainable contradiction to reserve liberty for some segments of the population while denying it to others.

Nor was the American Dream's promise of liberty ever confined to the borders of the United States. The framers of the Constitution considered its founding principle of human dignity to be universal in scope. During the modern era, in his widely read 1941 essay entitled "The American Century", publisher Henry Luce re-invigorated the notion that the Dream should be available to the entire world. People everywhere, Luce wrote, can benefit from a "love of freedom, a feeling for the equality of opportunity, a tradition of self-reliance and independence, and also of cooperation."[22]

Interestingly, although Luce's statement drew some criticism from those who worried about its imperialistic connotations (which Luce strenuously denied), it was not contested by mainstream commentators or leaders of either political party. In fact, the Democratic vice president, Henry Wallace, the most progressive politician of his day, wrote approvingly that Luce's vision "is almost precisely parallel" to Wallace's own view of America's responsibility to share the principles of freedom and democracy with the rest of humanity.[23] The world history of the next half century validated this bipartisan consensus on America's global role, as the United States helped extend freedom to millions of oppressed people by facilitating the defeat of fascism and communism.

We might expect, based on this history, that America's contributions to liberty at home and abroad would be a source of national pride that educators would be eager to pass along to students as a way to nurture civic purpose among them. In fact, this is exactly what I did expect when I convened a group of leading educators for a conference on education for American citizenship in June 2010.[24] The day's discussions, which revolved around the question of how to teach students about American identity and the American tradition, were thoughtful and informative. I gained many valuable insights from the presentations about the different ways in which diverse segments of the US population have construed American identity over the years. Together, the speakers made well-informed and convincing cases that there are "multiple narratives" in our national experience— some positive, others less so—that must be considered for an accurate view of what it has meant to be an American.

Yet, with some exceptions, few of the speakers that day took a position on *which* of these multiple narratives should be emphasized in educational programs that could foster civic understanding and purpose among our students. Most participants seemed hesitant to suggest a narrative that could promote pride in the American tradition or hope for the preservation of the American Dream. I believe that the general feeling in the conference, also widely shared among other educators today, is that there have been too many mistakes, broken promises, and other disappointments to recommend anything other than a complex, critically oriented program for the classroom.

Late in the proceedings, I offered the following statement: Young people will not become motivated to make any serious, long-term commitment to something unless they believe it to be worthwhile. When they are first learning about a new part of life, the young need something positive to believe in before they will make a commitment; and they need to care about something before they will become motivated to learn the skills necessary to carry out the commitment.

Citizenship is a *serious* commitment. It is essential that students make it, both for themselves and for the future of our democracy. But they will only do so if they learn to care about the fate of our society. This means developing an appreciation for the principles of liberty embodied in the American tradition and believing in the ideals envisioned by the elevated versions of the American Dream. Now this should *not* mean shielding students from the criticism that has been directed at the debatable actions the United States has taken in the past. But it *should* mean setting that criticism in the context of the undeniable gains in liberty and equality that American have achieved over the centuries

As examples from recent US history, I offered three cases in point that could be taught to students as a way to promote trust and attachment to American society: the civil rights movement that extended new rights to millions of citizens in the United States; the victories over totalitarianism (in particular, fascism, communism, and other militaristic despotisms) that have extended new freedoms to millions of subjugated people in Europe and Asia; and the post–World War II creation of a vibrant middle class that brought economic freedoms to millions of ordinary citizens as well as to immigrants coming to America in search of a better life. At the conference, my examples drew the kind of awkward silence that indicates you have said something that most people disagree with.

After the meeting, I asked a student who had mingled with the participants during a break if she knew what was going on. She told me she had the impression that few of them accepted my positive rendition of recent American history. Some, she said, may have felt that the success of the civil rights movement was due to courageous dissenters— and in any event, unjust racial gaps still exist. Further, the fall of communism without a single bullet could not be credited to any American actions or policies; and the American efforts had been marred by war-mongering rhetoric. In addition, our middle class is besieged, the American Dream itself is dead or dying, and China is about to supplant us in economic dominance.

From this bleak perspective, criticism rather than positivity is in order when we present the facts about our society to students. Of course, I had no reliable way of determining how many participants shared this kind of negativism regarding the past actions and future prospects of the United States. But this did appear to be the tone that prevailed in many of the views that people choose to express on that public occasion.

Where does this leave us in education today? Certainly the climate for fostering civic purpose among America's youth leaves a lot to be desired: It is hard to see how a young person could be willing to sacrifice for a society that offers no rational basis for hope, pride, or affection. Both in our schools and our civic discourse, we are failing to convey any reason for a young person to commit to American citizenship.

How long has it been since a respected public leader urged Americans to "ask not what your country can do for you but what you can do for your country"? When was the last time that one of our public leaders referred to America as a "shining city on a hill"? Young people listen for such messages. They welcome calls for their contributions, even ones that require effort and sacrifice. Yet in our time, the airwaves have gone silent on matters of national purpose, replaced by the incessant appeals to consumerism and other self-absorbed pursuits.

Voices of Young Americans Today

Before we get too discouraged, however, there is one more data point that we must consider: the mental and spiritual inclinations of American youth themselves. Here there is more than a little good news. As in every previous historical epoch, many young people are resilient, idealistic, and eager to devote themselves to higher causes (or, to quote from a source of wisdom from thousands of years ago—Aristotle—"they are hopeful, their lives are filled with expectation, they are more brave than persons of other ages, they are high-minded, and they choose to do what is noble rather than what is expedient").

And this is just what my research team has found in our interviews with diverse samples of young Americans today. As I discussed in the previous chapter, few young Americans aspire to civic leadership roles these days, and many are still searching for their purposes in life. Nevertheless, the embers of youthful idealism and hope still glow. If their pride in their American identity is fanned, the incipient devotion to their country can be brought to life as well.

It is especially interesting—and informative—to contrast what young Americans say about the American Dream with what they hear from those who influence educational trends today. Recall, for example, the sociologist's banishment of the Dream to "a place where anyone who builds a better mouse-trap can get rich"—a diminished and materialistic interpretation that is entirely in keeping with the conventional thinking in the field of education today. Compare this view, for insight and inspiration, with the more elevated vision of an eighteen-year-old student from Fairfield, California:

> I think the American Dream is that people can be who they are. Like freedom of religion, freedom of speech, freedom of action, and stuff. I do believe in that. People can be who they want to be. They shouldn't be influenced by the government, influenced by anyone else, other than themselves, to be themselves. . . . [In America we have] freedom to choose what job [we] want, freedom to speak or speak how [we] want, choose what religion [we] want to choose, all those kinds of freedoms.

An immigrant youth from India, who said he was "proud to say that I'm from that heritage and culture, but I'm proud of my American culture as well," told us that he saw the American Dream as presenting both opportunities and obligations, having a chance to get "a good job, make a good living, and uphold your duties to your country in all ways possible." He found this inspirational, particularly when he was feeling down: "Looking back at all this country has gone through, yeah, it inspires me." His capsule summary of the Dream's message was, "I think that it comes back to freedom of speech, freedom of expression, and the fact that if you really have a dream and you work hard, you can achieve it."

What about the girl, quoted just beneath the title of this chapter, whose history teacher had declared the Dream deceased? Fortunately, she proved that young people have minds of their own. This girl refused to be swayed by her teacher's negativism:

> I hear "American Dream," and I think the chance to pursue your dreams, the daring to be whoever you want to be. . . . Last year, the history teacher told us that the American Dream was dead because apparently we just work now, and we don't dream. I just—I didn't believe that at all. If we didn't dream, then we wouldn't be doing anything. We wouldn't be advancing as a society. Well, the whole class was just sort of silent, and he could tell that we didn't really agree with that, and then we had this big discussion about how we were dreaming and we were daring to be different people. It was amusing. Well, I guess it inspires me . . . that I can pursue my dreams, not just accept what's happening.

I do not wish to paint an overly rosy a picture. Too many young people have been influenced by the constant barrage of criticism that they are exposed to when they hear contemporary cultural discourse about the meaning and viability of the American Dream. Here is how one eighteen-year-old boy spoke about his American identity and his view of the Dream:

> I don't consider myself an American in any way. American dream, American lies. People from different places, they hear stories about the American dream, about money and a better life, (but no one tells them) how to achieve that American dream. . . . [I]t just doesn't fit in the American dream.

And a girl of the same age from the same school:

> I think that it's—excuse my language but—I think that the US government is like a drug dealer or a pimp. Because if you think about it, the US has different countries doing things for them, but they only break them off a little piece of money, and they use them, and manipulate them. They try to control them. Try looking up the definition of a pimp, and then you will see where I'm coming from. . . . I guess I'm not a true US citizen, or what America wants me to be, because America doesn't even abide by their own rules or their own expectations, so I don't know what a US citizen is. . . . I don't know what [the American Dream] would mean to me. I heard [the phrase] so many times. And it's crazy, and I don't know what it is. Everybody always says the American Dream, but I don't know what that is. When I think of American Dream, I think of beauty pageants for some reason. It's crazy.

What the American Dream means to young people today is more than a matter of passing cultural trivia. If the Dream means little, or if it is confined to its most base connotations of quick materialistic gain, we cannot deny that our society's

123

prospects have grown dimmer within our lifetimes. If, on the other hand, young Americans come to appreciate some of the deeper meanings that the American Dream has held for hopeful citizens over the centuries; if they come to understand the role of liberty in fostering this hope; if they learn that liberty does not come easily or automatically to any society, but requires particular social conditions and the dedication of citizens to maintain; and if they are educated to develop the virtues and the character required for living responsibly in a free society, *then* the American Dream will remain intact for them and for future generations to come.

EPILOGUE

[T]here is no truth more thoroughly established,
than that there exists . . . an indissoluble union
between virtue and happiness. —George Washington

The life of the nation is secure only while the nation is honest,
truthful and virtuous. —Frederick Douglas

The United States today faces many daunting challenges. At the time of this writing, some problems that Americans are worried about include high unemployment, a foreign war that shows few signs of ending, blatant greed and corruption on Wall Street, the weakening of the dollar, the waning of US economic competitiveness on the global stage, the divisiveness of political discourse, and international enemies who would gladly see the United States go up in flames. Many worry about the dwindling of natural resources and looming environmental disasters; others worry about the rise of vigorous but irate populist movements. Mainstream media stories cycle back and forth between such concerns on a daily basis, fomenting a climate of national anxiety that has many in the United States convinced that their country's time in the sun is past, that there will be no future "American Centuries."

So what else is new? Such concerns, and graver ones, have existed at practically every point in our history. Foreign enemies often have looked more formidable than any we face now: if there had been Las Vegas oddsmakers in the eighteenth century, they surely would have bet on the British; World War II looked perilous at the time; and after the Soviet Union acquired the hydrogen bomb, schoolchildren in the 1950s (I among them) practiced scurrying under our desks in anticipation of Russian attacks. The despoiling of the American environment has been lamented since the pastoral tales of James Fennimore Cooper, and previous economic hard times have been more severe for larger portions of the US population than anything on the horizon today. Through it all, Americans have proved to be resilient and courageous. As for populist anger, in the United States, because of the moderating effects of constitutional restraints, it generally has ended in constructive social change after the political processes of negotiation and reconciliation take hold.

Yet amidst the enduring cycle of recurring challenge and adaptation, one thing *is* new: we are now in danger of losing present and future generations of young Americans to the cause of preserving liberty. We have created this danger by neglecting to foster the civic virtues that motivate moral responsibility, civic participation, and personal sacrifice for the common good.

Of course, if asked, most adults in our society would claim that they are in favor of such things. Virtually all would say that they want their children to become good and responsible citizens. But civic virtue is not among the priorities of the education that we now provide to most American students. Listen to the speeches of our political leaders; read the mission statements of the funding agencies that provide support to our schools; and watch popular media presentations about reform efforts in education today. You may be surprised by what you see and hear. Rarely if ever in these influential circles will you hear an interest in civic virtue as an objective of education. Rarely if ever will you hear a concern for the development of our students' moral character. Rarely, in fact, will you hear a mention of the purposes that will guide our students' most important choices in life—even though such purposes have an impact on the very object of concern that is occupying the attention of political leaders these days, academic achievement. Compounding the folly, our educational neglect of virtue and civic purpose not only endangers the future of our free society but also weakens efforts to cultivate basic skills among our students. This is negligence, shortsightedness, and tunnel vision mixed together in a fatal brew.

The United States is a huge and many-faceted country. Any absolutist claims are bound to miss the whole story. At the present time, there are many positive social trends enhancing the developmental prospects of American youth. Volunteerism has risen enormously over the past decade or so, and many schools sponsor worthwhile community service programs. Some schools still take character education seriously, despite a lack of support or interest in this effort among education policy leaders. Some history teachers do a magnificent job of imparting a deep understanding of the American tradition; and in the best cases, students have access to history courses that place the American experience in the perspective of the other great world traditions.

All of these advantageous educational offerings are not only possible, they actually exist somewhere in the immense landscape of contemporary American society.

But they are not prominent parts of the landscape. We must look hard to find sure and stable cases of them. They rarely emerge from reports of school performance. Too often, as soon as a truly beneficial educational program in civic virtue is put in place, it falls apart from lack of support and exhaustion. There is an air of impermanence to even the best efforts, and the rest are sapped by feelings of futility and indifference. How much can we say we really value the mission of fostering virtue and character among students from all sectors of our society?

In the end, as I have argued throughout the present book, this question translates into a second one of equally grave consequence: How much do we value liberty in our society? If we understand the links between virtue and liberty with even a small fraction of the insights that the Founders of our democracy brought to bear on the matter, and if we feel a commitment to preserve for future generations the cherished legacy of liberty that has been granted us, our responsibilities are clear. We must open our schools, our homes, and our popular culture to expressions of virtue that can inform and inspire the finest possible civic education and character development of young people throughout our society.

NOTES

Introduction

1. Gary J. Schmitt et al., *High Schools, Civics, and Citizenship: What Social Studies Teachers Think and Do* (Washington, DC: American Enterprise Institute, 2010).
2. The classic study of parental attitudes on this matter is Steve Farkas and Jean Johnson, *A Lot to Be Thankful For: What Parents Want Children to Learn About America* (New York: Public Agenda, 1998). Teacher attitudes are documented in the 2010 AEI study referenced in Note 1.
3. Schmitt, *High Schools, Civics, and Citizenship,* 6.
4. Mark Bauerlein, *The Dumbest Generation: How the Digital Age Stupefies Young Americans and Jeopardizes Our Future (or, Don't Trust Anyone Under 30)* (New York: Jeremy P. Tarcher / Penguin, 2008).
5. William Damon, *The Path to Purpose: How Young People Find Their Calling in Life* (New York: Free Press, 2008).
6. *The Federalist* (New York: John Tiebout, 1799), 1:1, accessed January 4, 2011, http://www.loc.gov/rr/program/bib/ourdocs/federalist.html. Available in Prints & Photographs Division, Library of Congress; Reproduction Number: LC-USZ62-70508.
7. Eamonn Callan, "A Note on Patriotism and Utopianism: Response to Schrag," *Studies in Philosophy and Education* 18, no. 3 (1999): 197–201.

Chapter One

1. Peter Berkowitz, *Virtue and the Making of Modern Liberalism* (Princeton, NJ: Princeton University Press, 1999).

2. Jacob Needleman, *The American Soul: Rediscovering the Wisdom of the Founders* (New York: Jeremy P. Tarcher / Putnam, 2002).

3. James Q. Wilson, *The Moral Sense* (New York: Free Press, 1993); William Damon, "The Moral Development of Children," *Scientific American* 281, no. 2 (1999): 72–88; and Jonathan Haidt, *The Happiness Hypothesis: Finding Modern Truth in Ancient Wisdom* (New York: Basic Books, 2006).

4. Francis A. J. Ianni, *The Search for Structure: A Report on American Youth Today* (New York: Free Press, 1989); and William Damon, *The Youth Charter: How Communities Can Work Together to Raise Standards for All Our Children* (New York: Free Press, 1997).

5. In the early 1990s, homicide among teenagers had risen 124 percent from the prior decade, teen suicide had tripled, and every year saw more than a million teens becoming pregnant. See William Damon, *Greater Expectations: Overcoming the Culture of Indulgence in Our Homes and Schools* (New York: Free Press, 1995). Each of those trends has attenuated, although the problems have by no means disappeared.

6. William Damon, *The Path to Purpose: How Young People Find Their Calling in Life* (New York: Free Press, 2008).

7. Ibid.

8. Ibid., 423–52.

9. Christopher Peterson and Martin E. P. Seligman, *Character Strengths and Virtues: A Handbook and Classification* (Washington, DC: American Psychological Association, 2004).

10. Larry P. Nucci and Darcia Narvaez, *Handbook of Moral Character Education* (New York: Routledge, 2008).

11. Needleman, *The American Soul*.

12. Harvey C. Mansfield, "Liberty and Virtue in the American Founding," in *Never a Matter of Indifference: Sustaining Virtue in a Free Republic*, ed. Peter Berkowitz (Stanford, CA: Hoover Institution Press, 2003), 3–28.

13. Wilson, *The Moral Sense*; Damon, "The Moral Development of Children."

14. John C. Gibbs, *Moral Maturity: Measuring the Development of Sociomoral Reflection* (Hillsdale, NJ: L. Erlbaum Associates, 1991).

15. William Damon, *The Moral Child: Nurturing Children's Natural Moral Growth* (New York: Free Press, 1990).

16. Ibid.

17. Russell Muirhead, *Just Work* (Cambridge, MA: Harvard University Press, 2004).

18. Damon, *Greater Expectations*.

19. William Damon, *The Moral Advantage* (San Francisco: Berrett-Koehler, 2004); see also Damon, *The Path to Purpose*.

20. *Child Trends: Research to Improve Children's Lives*, 2009, accessed January 5, 2011, http://www.childtrends.org/index.cfm.
21. Andrew J. Cherlin, *The Marriage Go-round: The State of Marriage and the Family in America Today* (New York: Alfred A. Knopf, 2009).
22. Ibid.
23. Marshall Heyman, "Hackwork," *New Yorker*, August 31, 2009, 27–8.
24. Aletha C. Huston and John C. Wright, "Mass Media and Children's Development," in *Handbook of Child Psychology: The Sixth Edition (Vols. 1–4)*, ed. William Damon and Richard Lerner (New York: John Wiley & Sons, 2006), 999–1058.
25. Donald N. Wood, *The Unraveling of the West: The Rise of Postmodernism and the Decline of Democracy* (Westport, CT: Praeger, 2003); see also Wood, *Post-Intellectualism and the Decline of Democracy: The Failure of Reason and Responsibility in the Twentieth Century* (Westport, CT: Greenwood Publishing Group / Praeger, 1996).
26. Charles J. Sykes, *A Nation of Victims: The Decline of the American Character* (New York: St. Martin's Press, 1992).
27. William Damon, "Good? Bad? Or None of the Above? The Time-honored Unavoidable Mandate to Teach Character," *Education Next* 5, no. 2 (2005): 29–38.
28. Richard Arum et al., *Judging School Discipline: The Crisis of Moral Authority in American Schools.* (Cambridge, MA: Harvard University Press, 2003).
29. Donald L. McCabe, Linda K. Trevino, and Kenneth D. Butterfield, "Cheating in Academic Institutions: A Decade of Research," *Ethics & Behavior* 11, no. 3 (2001): 219–32.
30. Chester E. Finn, "Schooling," in *Never a Matter of Indifference: Sustaining Virtue in a Free Republic*, ed. Peter Berkowitz (Stanford, CA: Hoover Institution Press, 2003), 85–112.

Chapter Two

1. "The Marriage Index," Institute for American Values report, 2009, http://www.americanvalues.org/pdfs/IAV_Marriage_Index_09_25_09.pdf.
2. Linda J. Waite and Maggie Gallagher, *The Case for Marriage: Why Married People Are Happier, Healthier, and Better Off Financially* (New York: Doubleday, 2000), 67–76.
3. Cynthia Osborne and Sara McLanahan, "Partnership Instability and Child Well-Being," *Journal of Marriage and Family* 69 (2007): 1075–6.

4. Richard Arum and Doreet Preiss, "Law and Disorder in the Classroom: Emphasis on Student Rights Continues in Classrooms Even When the Court Begins to Think Otherwise," *Education Next* 9, no. 4 (Fall 2009): 58–66, http://educationnext.org/law-and-disorder-in-the-classroom/.

5. Ibid., 60.

6. Ibid., 58–66.

7. Ibid.

8. Ibid.

9. Ibid., 65.

10. Mark R. Lepper and David Greene, *The Hidden Costs of Reward: New Perspectives on the Psychology of Human Motivation* (Hillsdale, NJ: L. Erlbaum Associates, 1978); William Damon, *Greater Expectations: Overcoming the Culture of Indulgence in Our Homes and Schools* (New York: Free Press, 1995); and Joan E. Grusec, Jaqueline J. Goodnow, and Leon Kuczynski, "New Directions in Analyses of Parenting Contributions to Children's Acquisition of Values," *Child Development* 71, no. 1 (2000): 205–11.

11. William Damon, "The Moral Development of Children," *Scientific American* 281, no. 2 (1999): 72–88.

12. Donald L. McCabe, Linda K. Treviño, and Kenneth D. Butterfield, "Cheating in Academic Institutions: A Decade of Research," *Ethics & Behavior* 11, no. 3 (2001): 219–32.

13. Christina Hoff Sommers, "How Moral Education is Finding Its Way Back into America's Schools," in *Bringing in a New Era in Character Education*, ed. William Damon (Stanford, CA: Hoover Institution Press, 2002), 25. See Sommers's description of a teacher who held that, in a case of cheating, "it was the teacher who was immoral for having given the students such a burdensome assignment. . ."

14. Francie Grace, "Teachers Caught Cheating: Some Critics Blame Pressure of Standardized Testing." CBS News Online, October 28, 2003, http://www.cbsnews.com/stories/2003/10/28/national/main580355.shtml.

15. William Damon, *The Youth Charter: How Communities Can Work Together to Raise Standards for All Our Children* (New York: Free Press, 1997).

16. McCabe, Treviño, and Butterfield, "Cheating in Academic Institutions."

17. William Damon, ed., *Bringing in a New Era in Character Education* (Stanford, CA: Hoover Institution Press, 2002).

18. Steve Farkas and Jean Johnson, *A Lot to Be Thankful For: What Parents Want Children to Learn About America* (New York: Public Agenda, 1998).

19. My recounting of this incident relies on my far-from-perfect memory—in particular, the quotes from the parent are just my approximations, to the best of my recollections, of what the parent actually said.
20. See M. Killen and J. Smetana, eds., *Handbook of Moral Development* (Mahwah, NJ: L. Erlbaum Associates, 2006); and F. Oser, *Moralische Selbsbestimmung: Modelle Der Entwicklung und Erziehung im Wertebereich* (Berlin: Klett-Cotta, 2001).
21. William Damon, *The Moral Child: Nurturing Children's Natural Moral Growth* (New York: Free Press, 1990).
22. Marvin W. Berkowitz and Melinda C. Bier, *What Works in Character Education: A Research-driven Guide for Educators* (Washington, DC: Character Education Partnership, 2004).
23. Alfie Cohn, *What Does It Mean to Be Well Educated? And More Essays on Standards, Grading, and Other Follies* (Boston: Beacon Press, 2004).
24. James Davison Hunter, *The Death of Character: Moral Education in an Age Without Good or Evil* (New York: Basic Books, 2000).
25. Damon, *Bringing in a New Era.*
26. Social and Character Development Research Consortium, *Efficacy of Schoolwide Programs to Promote Social and Character Development and Reduce Problem Behavior in Elementary School Children (NCER 2011–2001)* (Washington, DC: National Center for Education Research, Institute of Education Sciences, US Department of Education, 2010), http://ies.ed.gov/ncer/pubs/20112001/index.asp.
27. Because of this assumption, not only matters of character development but also subjects such as art and music have been de-emphasized or eliminated from the school day in many of our public schools. Although that is an issue beyond the scope of this book, I doubt whether this is a sensible move even in an economic sense. The entertainment industry, which draws heavily on art and music skills, is one of the few manufacturing industries in the United States that steadily yields a positive balance of payments as well as high levels of employment.
28. Richard A. Stanhope, "Character education: A compilation of literature in the field from 1920 to 1991" (unpublished diss., University of Pittsburgh, 1992).
29. Kevin Ryan and David E. Purpel, *Moral Education: It Comes with the Territory* (New York: Basic Books, 1977).
30. Lawrence Arthur Cremin, *Traditions of American Education* (New York: Basic Books, 1977).

31. See, for example, Edward Wynne and Kevin Ryan, *Reclaiming Our Schools: A Handbook for Teaching Character, Academics, and Discipline* (Columbus, OH: Charles Merrill, 1992).
32. Lynn Cheney, "Whatever Happened to the Work Ethic?," *Wall Street Journal,* December 5, 1993; and William Damon, *The Path to Purpose: How Young People Find Their Calling in Life* (New York: Free Press. 2008).
33. Damon, *The Path to Purpose.*
34. Kara Miller, "My Lazy American Students," *The Boston Globe,* December 21, 2009.
35. Richard H. Hersh and John Merrow, eds., *Declining by Degrees: Higher Education at Risk* (New York: Palgrave Macmillan, 2005).

Chapter Three

1. Kevin Rathunde and Mihaly Csikszentmihalyi, "The Developing Person," in *Handbook of Child Psychology,* ed. Richard Lerner (New York: John Wiley & Sons, 2006), vol, 1, chap. 9.
2. Richard Dagger, *Civic Virtues: Rights, Citizenship, and Republican Liberalism* (New York: Oxford University Press, 1997).
3. This has been the case since the founding of the Republic and is rarely challenged, despite the obvious geographical fact that the United States comprises only about one-fifth of the American continent.
4. Philip Gleason, "American Identity and Americanization," in *Harvard Encyclopedia of American Ethnic Groups,* ed. Stephan Thernstrom (Cambridge, MA: Harvard University Press, 1980), 31–58.
5. Thierry Devos and Mahzarin H. Banaji, "American = White?," *Journal of Personality and Social Psychology* 88, no. 3 (2005): 447–66.
6. José Itzigohn, *Encountering American Faultlines: Race, Class, and the Dominican Experience in Providence* (New York: Russell Sage Foundation, 2009).
7. Tom Brokaw, *The Greatest Generation* (New York: Random House, 1998).
8. Doug McAdam, *Freedom Summer* (New York: Oxford University Press, 1988).
9. Peter Spiro, *Beyond Citizenship: American Identity after Globalization* (New York: Oxford University Press, 2007).
10. Harold Evans, *The American Century* (New York: Knopf, 1998), 6.
11. Kay Deaux, "To Be an American: Immigration, Hyphenation, and Incorporation," *Journal of Social Issues* 64, no. 4 (2008): 925–43.

12. Recently, political theorist Danielle Allen has introduced the notion of "wholeness"—as distinct from "oneness"—to convey a more integrated sense of American identity that retains recognition of diversity within; but this idea has not gained much popular traction. See Danielle Allen, *Talking to Strangers: Anxieties of Citizenship since Brown v. Board of Education* (Chicago: University of Chicago Press, 2004).
13. Evans, *The American Century*, especially 50–7.
14. Jacob Needleman, *The American Soul: Rediscovering the Wisdom of the Founders* (New York: Jeremy P. Tarcher / Putnam, 2002).
15. Evans, *The American Century*.
16. Ibid.
17. Martha Nussbaum, ed., "Patriotism and Cosmopolitanism," in *For Love of Country: Debating the Limits of Patriotism* (Boston: Beacon Press, 1996), 3–20.
18. Ibid., 6.
19. Amy Gutmann, "Democratic Citizenship," in *For Love of Country: Debating the Limits of Patriotism*, ed. Martha Nussbaum (Boston: Beacon Press, 1996), 67–68.
20. Michael Billig, *Banal Nationalism* (Thousand Oaks, CA: Sage Press, 1995), 7.
21. Robert Pinsky, "Eros against Esperanto," in Nussbaum, *For Love of Country*, 88.
22. Michael Walzer, "Spheres of Affection," in Nussbaum, *For Love of Country*, 125–7.
23. Michael W. McConnell, "Don't Neglect the Little Platoons," in Nussbaum, *For Love of Country*, 78–84.
24. William Damon, *The Path to Purpose: How Young People Find Their Calling in Life* (New York: Free Press, 2008).
25. The interviews were conducted as part of a series of studies that were supported by a number of foundations, including the Carnegie Corporation of New York, the John Templeton Foundation, the Thrive Foundation for Youth, and the Spencer Foundation. All conclusions from this program of research are that of the author and not of any of the foundations.
26. Supported in part by a grant from the Spencer Foundation. All conclusions are that of the author and not of the foundation.
27. Susan Verducci and William Damon, "The Outlooks of Today's Teens," in *Adolescents A to Z*, ed. Richard Lerner and Jacqueline Lerner (New York: Oxford University Press, 2000).
28. Damon, *The Path to Purpose*.
29. Chris Hedges, "35% of High School Seniors Fail National Civics Test," *New York Times*, November 21, 1999.

30. S. Keeter et al., "The 2002 Civic and Political Health of the Nation," CIRCLE (The Center for Information and Research on Civic Learning and Engagement), September 2002, http://www.civicyouth.org/research/products/Civic_Political_Health.

31. Diane Ravitch, "Tot Sociology: On What Happened to History in the Grade Schools," *The American Scholar* (Summer 1987): 343–54.

32. Hanna Schissler and Yasemin Nuhoglu Soysal, eds., *The Nation, Europe, and the World: Textbooks and Curricula in Transition* (New York: Berghahn, 2005).

33. Kerry J. Kennedy, Carole L. Hahn, and Wing-on Lee, "Constructing Citizenship: Comparing the Views of Students in Australia, Hong Kong, and the United States," *Comparative Education Review* 52 (2008): 53–91.

34. Karen Mundy and Lynn Murphy, "Transnational Advocacy, Global Civil Society? Emerging Evidence from the Field of Education," *Comparative Education Review* 45 (2001): 85–126.

35. Howard Zinn, *A People's History of the United States* (New York: HarperCollins, 2009).

36. See http://www.zinnedproject.org/.

37. Zinn, *A People's History*, 400–1.

38. Comment made by Heinz Werner, a leading developmental-psychology theorist, in the mid-twentieth century.

39. See http://www.zinnedproject.org/.

40. Diane Ravitch, *Consumer's Guide to High School History Textbooks* (Washington, DC: Thomas B. Fordham Foundation, 2004).

41. Frederick M. Hess, *Still at Risk: What Students Don't Know, Even Now* (Washington, DC: Common Core, 2008).

42. Ibid., 1.

43. Ibid., 3–4.

44. Beverly Kelly, "Turning the Page on Textbook Selection," *Ventura County (CA) Star*, April 27, 2010.

45. Ibid.

46. John Gershman, "'Disposition' Emerges as Issue at Brooklyn College," *New York Sun*, May 31, 2005, 1.

47. See http://www.ncate.org/documents/pdsStandards.pdf (NCATE Standards, 2001), 30. It has been reported [see the *Harvard Education Letter* 23, no. 4 (July/August 2007)] that NCATE removed the reference to social justice in June 2006, although as of this writing the 2001 document was still available online as the link offered under "Standards for Professional Development Schools."

48. The new standard reads: **Professional Dispositions.** Professional attitudes, values, and beliefs demonstrated through both verbal and non-verbal behaviors as educators interact with students, families,

colleagues, and communities. These positive behaviors support student learning and development. NCATE expects institutions to assess professional dispositions based on observable behaviors in educational settings. The two professional dispositions that NCATE expects institutions to assess are *fairness* and the belief that all students can learn. Based on their mission and conceptual framework, professional education units can identify, define, and operationalize additional professional dispositions.

Chapter Four

1. Seymour M. Lipset, *It Didn't Happen Here: Why Socialism Failed in the United States* (New York: W. W. Norton, 2000).
2. Karen Tumulty, "American Exceptionalism: An Old Idea and a New Political Battle" *Washington Post*, November 30, 2010.
3. Louis P. Masur, "The American Character," *Chronicle of Higher Education* B8 (January 16, 2009).
4. Christopher Jencks, "Reinventing the American Dream," *Chronicle of Higher Education* B6 (October 17, 2008).
5. See Needleman's discussion of the American emphasis on freedom to follow individual conscience, J. Needleman, *The American Soul* (New York: Jeremy P. Tarcher / Putnam, 2002).
6. William M. Rohe and Harry L. Watson, *Chasing the American Dream: New Perspectives on Affordable Homeownership* (Ithaca, NY: Cornell University Press, 2007).
7. Barbara Ehrenreich, *Bait and Switch: The Futile Pursuit of the American Dream* (New York: Metropolitan Books, 2005).
8. Arthur Levine, "Colleges and the Rebirth of the American Dream," *Chronicle of Higher Education* A72, July 11, 2010.
9. James T. Adams, *The Epic of America* (Boston: Little, Brown, 1933).
10. Richard Weiss, *The American Myth of Success: From Horatio Alger to Norman Vincent Peale* (New York: Basic Books, 1969).
11. Ehrenreich, *Bait and Switch.*
12. Heather Boushey, "Horatio Alger Is Dead," Center for Economic and Policy Research Economics Seminar Series, 2005, http://www.cepr.net/index.php/economics-seminar-series/.
13. Martin E. P. Seligman, *The Optimistic Child: Proven Program to Safeguard Children from Depression & Build Lifelong Resilience* (New York: Houghton Mifflin, 1999).
14. Andrew Delbanco, *The Real American Dream: A Meditation on Hope* (Cambridge, MA: Harvard University Press, 1999).
15. Ibid.

16. Alexis de Tocqueville, *Democracy in America*, trans. Henry Reeve (New York: Alfred Knopf, 1945), 2:318.
17. James McPherson, *For Causes and Comrades: Why Men Fought in The Civil War* (New York: Oxford University Press, 1997).
18. At the entrance of Harvard's Widener Library, built soon after World War I, stood a mural depicting a young soldier tight in the arms of the Angel of Death, with an inscription reading, "Happy is he who with one embrace grasps Victory and Death." Perhaps significantly, the mural was removed during a renovation at the beginning of the twenty-first century.
19. William Damon, *The Path to Purpose: How Young People Find Their Calling in Life* (New York: Free Press, 2008).
20. Robert D. Putnam, *Bowling Alone: The Collapse and Revival of American Community* (New York: Simon & Schuster, 2000).
21. de Tocqueville, *Democracy in America*.
22. Henry Luce, "The American Century," *Life Magazine*, February 1941. Reprinted in Michael J. Hogan, ed. *The Ambiguous Legacy* (Cambridge, UK: Cambridge University Press, 1999).
23. Alan Brinkley, *The Publisher* (New York: Alfred A. Knopf, 2010).
24. The conference was held in New York City on June 5, 2010, and was supported by a grant from the John Templeton Foundation. A conference report can be found on the Stanford Center on Adolescence Web site, at http://coa.stanford.edu.

ABOUT THE AUTHOR

William Damon is a professor of education at Stanford University, director of the Stanford Center on Adolescence, and a senior fellow at the Hoover Institution. Before coming to Stanford, he was University Professor at Brown University. For the past twenty years, Damon has written on character development at all ages of human life. His books include *The Moral Child* (1990); *Some Do Care: Contemporary Lives of Moral Commitment* (1992) (with Anne Colby); *Greater Expectations: Overcoming the Culture of Indulgence in Our Homes and Schools* (1995); *The Youth Charter: How Communities Can Work Together to Raise Standards for All Our Children* (1997); *Good Work: When Excellence and Ethics Meet* (2001) (with Howard Gardner and Mihaly Csikszentmihalyi); *Bringing in a New Era in Character Education* (2002); *Noble Purpose* (2003); *The Moral Advantage* (2004); and *The Path to Purpose* (2008). Damon was founding editor of *New Directions for Child and Adolescent Development* and is editor in chief of *The Handbook of Child Psychology* (1998 and 2006 editions). He is a member of the National Academy of Education.

**BOYD AND JILL SMITH TASK FORCE
ON VIRTUES OF A FREE SOCIETY**

The Boyd and Jill Smith Task Force on Virtues of a Free Society examines the evolution of America's core values, how they are threatened, and what can be done to preserve them. The task force's aims are to identify the enduring virtues and values on which liberty depends; chart the changes in how Americans have practiced virtues and values over the course of our nation's history; assess the ability of contemporary associations and institutions—particularly schools, family, and religion—to sustain the necessary virtues; and discuss how society might nurture the virtues and values on which its liberty depends.

The core membership of this task force includes Peter Berkowitz, David Brady, Gerard V. Bradley, James W. Ceaser, William Damon, Robert P. George, Tod Lindberg, Harvey C. Mansfield, Russell Muirhead, Clifford Orwin, and Diana Schaub.

INDEX